THE VETERANS CEMETERIES OF TEXAS

Number 161
Williams-Ford Texas A&M University
Military History Series

THE VETERANS CEMETERIES OF TEXAS

Michael Lee Lanning

Texas A&M University Press
College Station

First edition

This paper meets the requirements of ANSI/NISO Z39.48–1992 (Permanence of Paper).
Binding materials have been chosen for durability.
Manufactured in the United States of America

Library of Congress Cataloging-in-Publication Data

Names: Lanning, Michael Lee, author.
Title: The veterans cemeteries of Texas / Michael Lee Lanning.
Other titles: Williams-Ford Texas A&M University military history series; no. 161.
Description: First edition. | College Station: Texas A&M University Press, [2018] | Series: Williams-Ford Texas A&M University military history series; number 161 | Includes bibliographical references and index.
Identifiers: LCCN 2017050612 | ISBN 9781623496487 (hardcover (printed case): alk. paper)
Subjects: LCSH: National cemeteries—Texas—History. | National cemeteries—Texas—Directories. | Veterans—Services for—Texas. | Veterans—Monuments—Texas. | Soldiers' bodies, Disposition of—Texas. | United States. National Cemetery Administration—Rules and practice. | Military funerals—United States.
Classification: LCC UB394.T4 L36 2018 | DDC 976.4—dc23 LC record available at https://lccn.loc.gov/2017050612

TO TEXAS VETERANS—
PAST, PRESENT, AND FUTURE

DIANA LYNN
KEMP
FEB 24 1958
APR 29 2010
WIFE OF
GEORGE O
KEMP JR
SGT USA
IN LOVING
MEMORY
RONALD L
STANSBERRY
SP4
US ARMY
VIETNAM
APR 24 1952
MAY 15 2010
IN THE HANDS
GARY
CRANE
GILL
SSG
US ARMY
VIETNAM
MAY 10 1939
ROSCOE
POOL
PFC
US ARMY
KOREA
NOV 23 1932
MAY 3 2010
LOVING HUSBAND
AND FATHER
CARNIE
DELTON
BERRY
PL SGT
US MARINE CORPS
WORLD WAR II
APR 4 1921
APR 23 2010
ALWAYS BELOVED

Contents

THE VETERANS CEMETERIES OF TEXAS

The muffled drum's sad roll has beat
The soldier's last tattoo;
No more on Life's parade shall meet
That brave and fallen few.
On Fame's eternal camping-ground
Their silent tents are spread,
And Glory guards, with solemn round
The bivouac of the dead.

—Theodore O'Hara (1820–1867)

Introduction

Since its very beginnings, the state of Texas has offered up its sons and daughters in defense of its borders as well as those of the United States, and these heroes have stood against threats and tyranny around the world. Texas soldiers, sailors, airmen, marines, and coastguardsmen have unselfishly answered their state's and country's call and have expected little in return. Because of the faithful service of its veterans, the United States has remained the bright beacon of freedom and liberty to the oppressed around the world.

Texas veterans—those who fell in battle, those who survived their war to return home, those who maintained the peace and prevented actual combat—all are well deserving of their small patch of ground for their grave. For that reason, the military and government has long provided a benefit—the last entitlement—for its veterans. A place for their last formation and final parade.

Charged with ensuring this final entitlement is the Department of Veterans Affairs, which is responsible for managing and maintaining the national cemeteries for those service members who elect interment in those designated spaces. Today Texas veterans lie in VA and state cemeteries from El Paso to Houston and from Mission to Abilene in final perfect formations and on permanent eternal parade to honor their service and their country.

The United States of America and the Lone Star Republic of Texas did not secure their independence in the courtroom, in the churchyard, or in the classroom. They earned their independence on the battlefields of Saratoga and Yorktown and at the Alamo and at San Jacinto. When the two countries united as one, they stood together to oppose incursions from Mexico. Although Texas seceded from the Union during the American Civil War, Texans fought on both sides in the conflict that ultimately reunited the states and preserved the Union.

During the post–Civil War years, Texas played an important role in the Indian Wars that helped push the borders of the United States westward. Texas and Texans then significantly contributed to the United States' victory in the Spanish American War of 1898. Since that time, in both world wars, in Korea and Vietnam, and in the more recent conflicts in the Mid-East, Texas has offered its land and ports for army, navy, marine corps, air force, and coast guard installations.

During the American colonial period and in the early years of the independent United States, soldiers killed in battle were buried where they fell or in nearby churchyard or village cemeteries. Losses were significant in these early fights, but not nearly so much as when the North and South opposed each other in the Civil War. The large number of battlefield casualties—from combat, accidents, and disease—created a need for a formal system of cemeteries for the burial of the dead.

On July 17, 1862, the US Congress passed legislation that authorized President Abraham Lincoln to purchase "cemetery grounds" for use as national burial sites for "the soldiers who shall have died in the service of the country." Fourteen cemeteries were established that first year, and by 1870 more than 300,000 Union dead had been buried in seventy-three national cemeteries. In 1873 all honorably discharged veterans became eligible for burial. During the latter years of the nineteenth century, the government added more national cemeteries near military posts on the western frontier. By 1900 the quartermaster general of the US Army was managing eighty-three national cemeteries with 342,242 internments as well as eight temporary cemeteries in the Philippines, Cuba, and Puerto Rico.

Following World War I, the US Congress established the American Battle Monuments Commission to maintain burial grounds overseas for US service members who died in the conflict. During World War II Congress increased their number to twenty-four.

In the 1930s Congress again took action to further provide for US veterans after their deaths by procuring land for new cemeteries near major metropolitan areas, including Baltimore, Minneapolis, New York, San Diego, and San Francisco. This legislation also provided the first veterans cemetery in Texas with the facility near downtown San Antonio.

In 1973 the supervision of the national cemeteries was transferred from the Department of the Army to the Veterans Administration (now the Department of Veterans Affairs). Over the years the number of national military cemeteries has grown to 141 facilities. Two of these—Arlington National Cemetery and the Soldiers' and Airmen's Home National Cemetery in Washington, DC—are administered by the Department of the Army. The Department of the Interior's National Park Service continues to administer fourteen of the cemeteries.

In the latter part of the twentieth century and the early years of the twenty-first, Congress passed laws establishing a dozen new cemeteries—including the one at Dallas–Fort Worth. More than 3 million people, including veterans of every American war and conflict as well as family members, are buried in national cemeteries consisting of more than 17,000 acres of land. Another 23 million veterans living today are eligible for burial. Veterans with discharges other than dishonorable, their spouses, and dependent children qualify for a space in national cemeteries. Those who die while on active duty are also eligible. (Detailed eligibility requirements are in Appendixes A and B.)

Secretary of State Colin Powell, then a general acting as the chairman of the Joint Chiefs of Staff, spoke at a Memorial Day ceremony at Arlington National Cemetery on November 11, 1989. He said, "The nation owes a great debt to its veterans, whose service to the nation spans every decade, every year, every day of our country's existence. Through untold courage and sacrifice, America's veterans have secured the liberty which the founding fathers sought to establish here in the new world. Whenever and wherever the nation has called—in times of darkness and danger as well as in times of peace and prosperity—America's veterans have been there. Veterans have proudly carried the torch of liberty for all to see."

On January 28, 2003, Secretary Powell said at the World Economic Forum at Davos, Switzerland, "We have gone forth from our shores repeatedly over the last hundred years and put wonderful young men and women at risk, many of whom lost their lives, and we have asked nothing except enough ground to bury them in, and otherwise we have returned home to seek our own lives in peace."

There are six national veterans cemeteries in Texas, but Texans have gone the extra measure by funding the purchase of land for four additional state facilities. In 2001, 75 percent of the state's voters passed a constitutional amendment approving Proposition 7. The amendment enabled the Texas Veterans Land Board to sell up to $500 million in bonds to fund land purchases for cemeteries as well as home mortgage loans to veterans. (Details of state cemeteries are covered in Part II.) Today there are more than 1.7 million living veterans in the state of Texas—the second-largest number of any state. More than 12,000 veterans are laid to rest annually in Texas veterans cemeteries.

The national and state sites share standards, traditions, and commonalities. The six VA cemeteries in Texas are administered and operated by US government employees; the four state cemeteries are administrated by the Texas Veterans Land Office and operated by the Premier Cemetery Service Corporation (details in Appendix C). All ten facilities comply with the regulations and guidelines of the Department of Veterans Affairs National Cemetery Administration. Other than the signs at their entranceways that identify them as either a VA or state cemetery, there is no difference in operation or appearance.

At the entrance of each cemetery, with the exceptions of those in San Antonio and Kerrville, a visitor center, staffed by cemetery employees and community volunteers, provides information and assistance. Information about the San Antonio and Kerrville facilities is available at the Fort Sam Houston Visitors Center.

The flags of the United States and the State of Texas occupy prominent positions in each cemetery. The flags of the US Army, Air Force, Navy, Marine Corps, and Coast Guard fly at each location. Another similarity is display of metal tablets with part or all of the poem *Bivouac of the Dead* by Theodore O'Hara (for the complete poem, see Appendix D).

Although not written by a Texan, the poem shows the great influence the state had on its origin. When the United States declared war on Mexico in response to a boundary dispute between

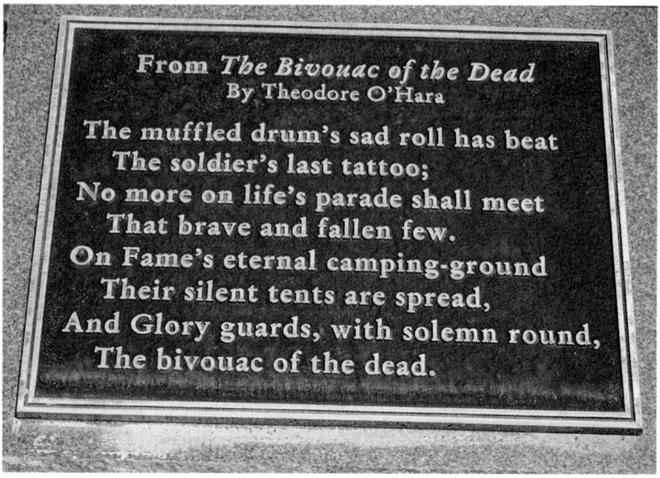

the two countries, regular and volunteer army units rushed to the border. Included was O'Hara, who rose to the rank of brevet brigadier general before the end of the conflict. There is some debate about just when O'Hara wrote *Bivouac*, but it is generally accepted that he wrote it to honor infantry and cavalry troops from his native Kentucky who fell at the Battle of Buena Vista near Monterrey, Mexico, on February 23, 1847.

O'Hara read his poem at several funerals of veterans after the war; it was first published in the *Frankfort Yeoman* in 1850. In 1855, O'Hara rejoined the US Army and served in Texas fighting Native Americans. At the outbreak of the Civil War in 1861, O'Hara joined the Confederate Army and served throughout the war. He died in 1867 and was buried in Columbus, Georgia. When his remains were moved to the Kentucky State Cemetery in 1874, Sgt. Henry T. Stanton read the poem at his old friend's reinterment. He said, "O'Hara, in giving utterance to this song, became at once the builder of his own monument and the author of his own epitaph."

Portions of *Bivouac*, particularly the conclusion of the first stanza—"On Fame's eternal camping-ground/Their silent tents are spread/That Glory guards, with silent round/The Bivouac of the dead"—began to appear at Confederate cemeteries before the war concluded. This practice spread to northern cemeteries after the conflict, including to Arlington National Cemetery shortly after it opened in 1864. O'Hara, because of his service on the rebel side, did not receive credit for its authorship at that cemetery at the time.

Over the years, portions of the poem were reproduced on painted boards at emerging veterans cemeteries. In 1881–1882 cast-iron tablets of the poem were fabricated at the War Department's Rock Island Arsenal, Illinois, with the stated purpose being "to take the place of notices and verses on painted signboards which have become unsightly and were too costly to renew as frequently as required." By the early 1930s, however, cemeteries had removed most of the tablets because of wear and continued concerns over O'Hara's service to the Confederacy. In the fall of 2001, the National Cemetery Administration began an initiative to install cast aluminum tablets of the poem, or portions thereof, in all the existing and future national cemeteries. The Texas state veterans cemeteries follow this initiative.

Another monument found in the national and state veterans cemeteries is a tablet of the Gettysburg Address. On November 19, 1863, President Abraham Lincoln made a brief, two-minute speech at the dedication of the Gettysburg National Cemetery to commemorate the battle of the previous summer. Over the following years, the address was posted at cemeteries across the country. On the bicentennial of Lincoln's birth in February 2009, the National Cemetery Administration took action to restore existing Gettysburg Address monuments and to erect new ones where they did not exist.

In a later address, President Lincoln also provided what would become the motto of the Department of Veterans Affairs and words that today appear on VA headquarters and on associated documents. With the Civil War nearing an end, Lincoln made his second inaugural address on March 4, 1865. The president orated on the moral and religious implications of the conflict

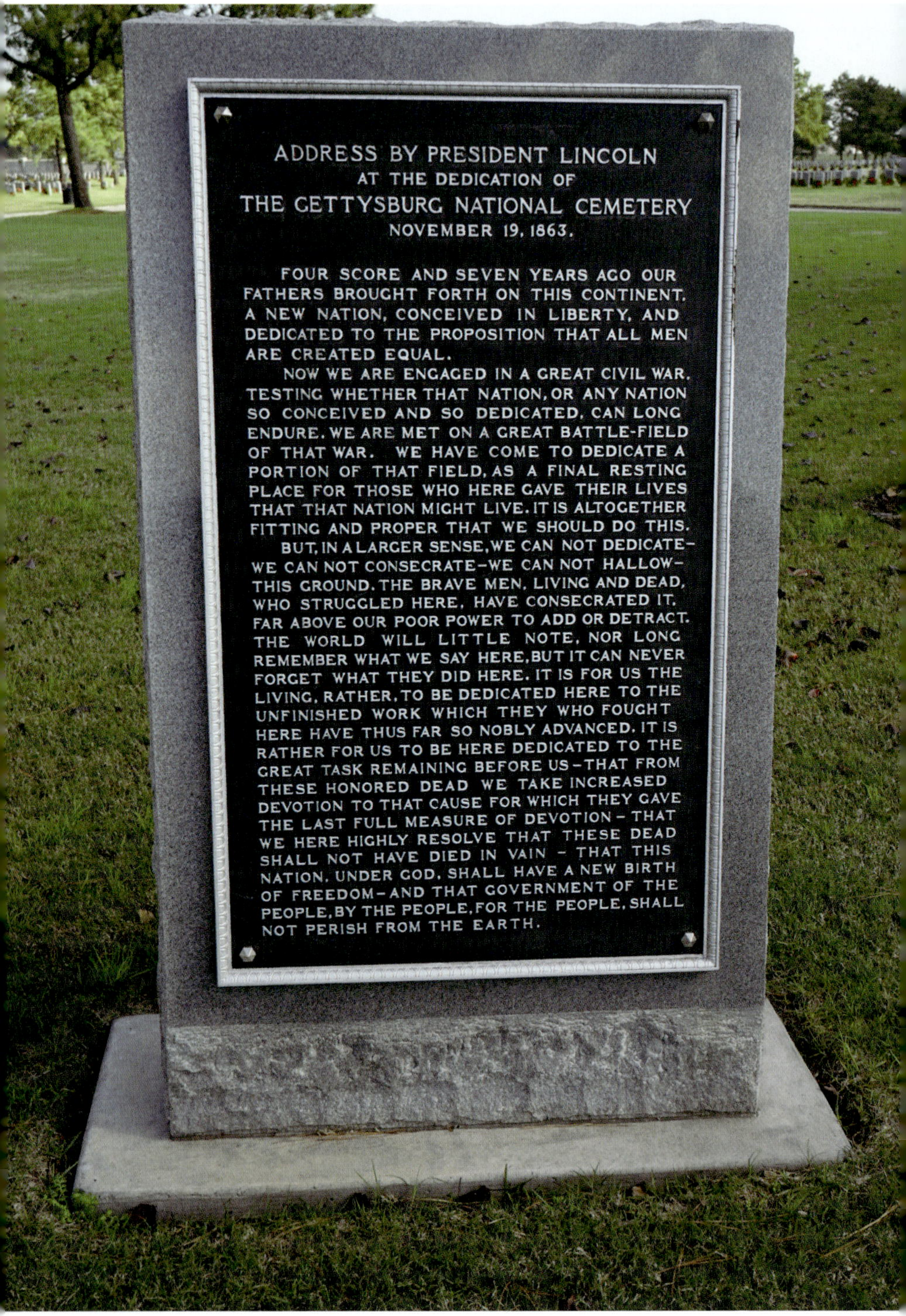
ADDRESS BY PRESIDENT LINCOLN
AT THE DEDICATION OF
THE GETTYSBURG NATIONAL CEMETERY
NOVEMBER 19, 1863.
FOUR SCORE AND SEVEN YEARS AGO OUR FATHERS BROUGHT FORTH ON THIS CONTINENT, A NEW NATION, CONCEIVED IN LIBERTY, AND DEDICATED TO THE PROPOSITION THAT ALL MEN ARE CREATED EQUAL.
NOW WE ARE ENGAGED IN A GREAT CIVIL WAR, TESTING WHETHER THAT NATION, OR ANY NATION SO CONCEIVED AND SO DEDICATED, CAN LONG ENDURE. WE ARE MET ON A GREAT BATTLE-FIELD OF THAT WAR. WE HAVE COME TO DEDICATE A PORTION OF THAT FIELD, AS A FINAL RESTING PLACE FOR THOSE WHO HERE GAVE THEIR LIVES THAT THAT NATION MIGHT LIVE. IT IS ALTOGETHER FITTING AND PROPER THAT WE SHOULD DO THIS.
BUT, IN A LARGER SENSE, WE CAN NOT DEDICATE-WE CAN NOT CONSECRATE-WE CAN NOT HALLOW-THIS GROUND. THE BRAVE MEN, LIVING AND DEAD, WHO STRUGGLED HERE, HAVE CONSECRATED IT, FAR ABOVE OUR POOR POWER TO ADD OR DETRACT. THE WORLD WILL LITTLE NOTE, NOR LONG REMEMBER WHAT WE SAY HERE, BUT IT CAN NEVER FORGET WHAT THEY DID HERE. IT IS FOR US THE LIVING, RATHER, TO BE DEDICATED HERE TO THE UNFINISHED WORK WHICH THEY WHO FOUGHT HERE HAVE THUS FAR SO NOBLY ADVANCED. IT IS RATHER FOR US TO BE HERE DEDICATED TO THE GREAT TASK REMAINING BEFORE US-THAT FROM THESE HONORED DEAD WE TAKE INCREASED DEVOTION TO THAT CAUSE FOR WHICH THEY GAVE THE LAST FULL MEASURE OF DEVOTION - THAT WE HERE HIGHLY RESOLVE THAT THESE DEAD SHALL NOT HAVE DIED IN VAIN - THAT THIS NATION, UNDER GOD, SHALL HAVE A NEW BIRTH OF FREEDOM-AND THAT GOVERNMENT OF THE PEOPLE, BY THE PEOPLE, FOR THE PEOPLE, SHALL NOT PERISH FROM THE EARTH.

and concluded with encouragement for the nation to rebuild and reconcile. He said: "With malice toward none, with charity for all, with firmness in the right as God gives us to see the right, let us strive on to finish the work we are in, to bind up the nation's wounds, to care for him who shall have borne the battle and for his widow, and his orphan, to do all which may achieve and cherish a just and lasting peace among ourselves and with all nations."

The words "to care for him who shall have borne the battle and for his widow, and his orphan" affirmed Lincoln's desire for the country to care for its veterans and their families. These words became the official motto of the VA in 1958. Today metal plaques containing the phrase flank the entrance to the headquarters of the Department of Veterans Affairs in Washington, DC.

The most distinctive aspect of veterans cemeteries—and the one that imparts a lasting memory for visitors—is the row upon row of headstones aligned with military precision. While each cemetery has its own distinct layout and design, all have neat uniform rows of headstones marking the graves of our country's finest individuals. Indeed the bivouac of the dead appear to lie forever in their final formation and at parade ready.

There are no graveside services in either the VA or state cemeteries. Rather, services are held in committal shelters that are on the outer edges of the burial sites. Upon completion of the committal service, the casket or urn is moved to the gravesite or columbarium.

The VA and state cemeteries offer several burial and marker options. These include a full-casketed burial, in-ground burial of cremated remains, a columbarium niche for cremated remains, or the scattering of ashes in a memorial garden. For markers, the VA provides either granite or marble upright stones or the choice of flat bronze, granite, or marble headstones for in-ground burials. Marble and bronze covers are available for columbaria niches. Upright headstones are 42 inches long, 13 inches wide, and 4 inches thick. They weigh approximately 230 pounds. Flat bronze markers are 24 inches long and 12 inches wide with a ¾-inch rise. They weigh 18 pounds. Flat granite or marble markers are 24 inches long, 12 inches wide, and 4 inches thick. They weigh approximately 130 pounds. Bronze niche markers are 8½ inches long and 5½ inches wide with a 7⁄16-inch rise. The weight is approximately 3 pounds.

HAROLD A
INNES
CPL
US ARMY
WORLD WAR II
APR 14 1922
JAN 5 2010
LOVING HUSBAND
DAD GRANDPA
AND GGPA
JERRY LYNN
DAVIS Sr
SFC
US ARMY
VIETNAM
JUL 10 1939
OCT 28 2008
MSM AM ARCOM
DEVOTED HUSBAND
LOVING FATHER
TRACY
LEE
MARTIN
SGT
US AIR FORCE

WILLIAM
EUGENE
FREDRICK
BILLY
JOE
LEE
US AIR FORCE
KOREA
DEC 2 1935
MAY 19 2016
HE LIVED
WITH HONOR

Grave markers are ordered and set by the cemetery at no cost to the veteran's family. Along with the surrounding grounds, the markers are constantly maintained to ensure their stability and uniformity. When single markers or rows of markers get out of alignment due to soil or moisture conditions, they are reset.

The VA closely regulates the engravings on headstones. Mandatory items on markers include the deceased's legal name, branch of service, year of birth, year of death, and the section and grave numbers. Optional items include the month and date of birth and death, the highest rank attained, decorations received, and the place or era of war service (such as World War II, Korea, or Vietnam). Additional items may also be included, such as a nickname, term of endearment, or military or civilian credentials or accomplishments (doctor or reverend). Also allowed are special unit designations, such as Seabees, Women Army Corps, or Army Nurse Corps.

Sixty religious emblems are authorized on the markers as well, ranging from the more common Christian cross and the Star of David to the more obscure Aaronic Order Church and Wiccan. Veterans and/or families also have the option of requesting that no religious symbol be engraved on the headstone. (A complete illustrated list of authorized religious symbols is in Appendix E.)

Gravesites are selected by the cemetery staff based on the next available space for the selected type of burial. Liners or vaults for all graves are provided. The vaults and graves are of sufficient size for the interment of a spouse at a later date.

Military funeral honors, including a firing squad and a bugler, are coordinated by the family's funeral home or directly by the cemetery staff. They are provided by Department of Defense units or Veterans Service Organizations in nearby communities. A US flag is provided at no cost to accompany the cremation urn or to drape the casket. This flag is presented to family members after the funeral. The family has the option of keeping the flag or donating it back to the cemetery to be flown in an avenue of flags on patriotic holidays.

VA regulations regarding headstones are strict. Private headstones are not allowed, though those in place in the older cemeteries that mark graves there before uniform VA regulations were enacted do remain. However, in addition to the upright and flat headstones that are permitted, group burial markers can be found throughout most of the cemeteries—especially the older ones. These markers stand over the burial sites of groups of service personnel who perished in a common battle or accident. Most of these are from air crashes in which recovered remains could not be individually identified. With the advances in science and DNA testing, group burials are becoming memorials to the past.

Central Texas Fallen Heroes Memorial Committee Founding Members
Patrick Turck - President
Jack St. John - Vice President
Amanda Dejournett - Secretary/Treasurer
Dave Crawford · Raul & Julia Villaronga · Ursula Pirtle
Linnie & Jessica Blankenbecler · Inge Colton · Gala Higginbottom
Special Thanks
Killeen Monument Company · Jack Welch/CHAMPS · City of Killeen
Mary Bourdon · Texas Veterans Land Board · VFW 9192 - Guadalupe Lopez
Jack Chapman/Cosper Construction · Central Texas Community

Each of the cemeteries also has areas where veterans' organizations and other groups can place metal or stone plaques and memorials to commemorate certain groups, units, campaigns, or other military events. These markers are spread out in the older cemeteries while they are restricted to certain areas, such as Memorial Walks, in the newer ones, including the four Texas state facilities. Memorial stone benches are also allowed when they honor the military service by individuals.

Three times a year all the grave and niche sites are honored in a uniform manner. For Memorial Day and Veterans Day, volunteers place a small US flag on each site a week or two before the holiday and they remain for a similar time afterward. This tradition began soon after the first VA cemeteries opened when families and friends placed flags on graves to mark these special holidays. It was not until the late twentieth century, however, that volunteer organizations acquired and placed flags for every veteran's last resting place.

During the Christmas and New Year season, volunteers also ensure that each grave and niche site is decorated with a holiday wreath. In 1992, Morrill Worcester, owner of the Worcester Wreath Company in Maine, had an excess of holiday wreaths. Remembering a visit to Arlington National Cemetery as a boy, he contacted cemetery officials about contributing the wreaths. Over the following years, volunteer organization across the country, including Texas, formed nonprofit organizations to solicit funds and workers so that each veteran's grave would have a colorful wreath to mark the season.

No place is more serene, calmer, or quieter than our national and state veterans cemeteries, and no one is more worthy of such appropriate surroundings than our military veterans. Stunningly beautiful, yet humbling, the national cemeteries in Texas honor veterans who have been laid to rest under long rows of military headstones. This hallowed ground, the bivouac of the dead, is a small but important tribute to the millions of veterans who came forward to defend our country's freedom.

Unlike some civilian cemeteries that still restrict burials to practitioners of certain religions—and unlike those racially segregated graveyards from the past—VA and state veterans cemeteries unite all veterans side by side as equals under the flag of the country they served with in uniform. It is common for veterans to say that it "will be an honor to be buried among fellow comrades."

Since its admission to the Union, Texas has contributed manpower and other support to preserve our country's liberty and independence. Today many of its veterans lie under marble and bronze headstones in national cemeteries across the state. A walk through these burial grounds is a journey across the history of Texas and of the United States. This is the story about the gravesites that honor Texans who lie in hallowed ground.

The hundreds of thousands of our veterans who are buried in our national and state cemeteries are the men and women who have fought our country's wars and defeated our enemies as well as those who served to maintain the peace and to continue to provide the beacon of freedom to the rest of the world. Most of their names and stories are known only to their families and close friends, yet all are notable for their selfless service and sacrifice. At the end of each chapter of this book is information on the ultra-heroes—those who earned the Medal of Honor—along with those individuals who gained fame in uniform or in civilian life. Despite this recognition, death and burial in our national and state cemeteries bring an equality to all our veterans in the long rows of headstones that mark the graves of those who proudly wore the uniform of their country.

UNITED STATES ARMY
1775

PART I

National VA Cemeteries in Texas

U S
NATIONAL CEMETERY
OPEN EVERY DAY
8-AM TO 5-PM

San Antonio National Cemetery

San Antonio, Texas

The San Antonio National Cemetery is the oldest in Texas and one of the earliest official final resting places for veterans in the United States. San Antonio de Bexar Presidio was established in 1718 and became the capital of Spanish Texas in 1778. Along with its governing responsibilities, the town became the center of military support and operations in the area—and has continued that role through today. During the Mexican Revolution of 1810, San Antonio officials sided with the rebels led by Father Miguel Hidalgo. They were initially successful in placing their Spanish officials under arrest. After only a month, however, the Royalist recaptured San Antonio and destroyed much of the town and executed many of the rebels.

San Antonio rebuilt but remained a center of unrest and violence. The Siege of Bexar took place in December 1835, followed by the battle and fall of the Alamo on March 6, 1836. When Texas finally won its independence from Mexico after the Battle of San Jacinto on April 21, the area was formed into Bexar County with

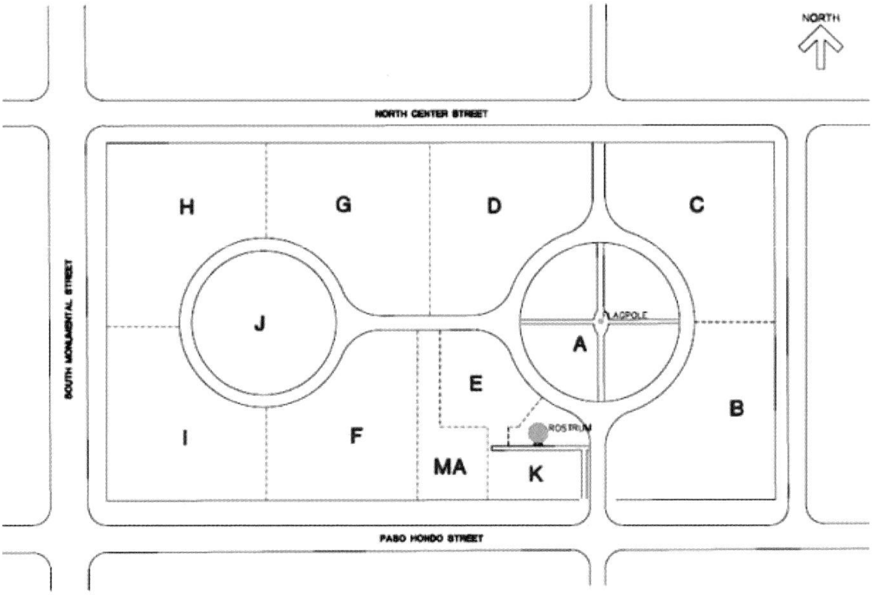

San Antonio as its seat of government. When Texas joined the Union in 1845, the US Army chose San Antonio as its military center for administration and supply for its operations against the Native Americans on the western frontier. San Antonio continued that mission during the Mexican War as its permanent population grew to more than 8,000 residents by 1860.

Local militias took control of the US facilities and arsenal even before Texas seceded from the Union to join the Confederacy in 1861. During the Civil War the town continued to serve as a Confederate depot.

Prior to and during the Civil War, soldiers who died or were killed on duty in the immediate San Antonio area were buried in the town's cemetery, located to the east of the Alamo and downtown. The City of San Antonio donated the original burial ground for many soldiers, consisting of 1.89 acres, to the United States for a veterans cemetery in 1867—one of the earliest other than those located on or near Civil War battlefields. The original deed for this transaction was apparently lost and never officially recorded. San Antonio executed a new deed on April 14, 1871, that

made the transfer official. In 1884 the United States purchased 1.75 additional acres from the city to complete the boundaries of the burial grounds. The national cemetery is now surrounded by civilian graveyards that prevent any further expansion.

Interments began soon after the veterans cemetery opened its gates in December 1867. The first burials were veterans' remains from San Antonio cemeteries as well as those at current and former military installations at Indianola, Austin, and other frontier outposts. More than 100 of these remains were identified while 314 were buried as unknowns in a common grave in Section H of the cemetery. A marker was erected at the site in 1912 with the simple inscription "To the Unknown Dead." A brass plaque was added in 1992 that states, "To the honored dead buried here in the eighteenth century, this monument honors 85 soldiers who died in the service of their country during the Indian Wars and were recently identified through research at Fort Concho National Landmark, San Angelo, Texas." A list of the 85 soldiers by name, unit, and birth and death date follow.

An inspector of national cemeteries filed a report on February 6, 1871, that said, "The remains of some of the officers of the Army, who died in San Antonio years ago, have recently been exhumed and re-interred here." The report also stated that graves were marked with ten-inch-square, two-feet-long limestone blocks that were placed flush with the top of the grave. The inspector noted

that the stone was soft, easy to work, and much more durable than the wooden markers previously used. Along with these standardized limestone markers, the cemetery contains more than 250 private markers—more than any other of the Texas veterans facilities.

The design of the cemetery has changed little since the 1870s. Its main entrance on Paso Hondo Street is composed of a double wrought-iron gate flanked on both sides by smaller pedestrian gates, also known as lichgates. In 1939 a four-foot-high stone wall was built enclosing the cemetery and separating it from the civilian burial ground to the north. The only structure on the grounds is an octagonal rostrum located just to the west of the main gate that was constructed in 1890 of stone blocks with a wrought-iron railing and a decorative staircase. It originally had a metal roof supported by eight columns, but they were removed in 1957.

Two circular burial areas dominate the eastern and western halves of the cemetery with a connecting cross-axis in the center. The cemetery's flagpole stands in the center of the eastern circle above many of the larger, private grave markers. Other graves fill in all other available space. By 1990, there were 3,161 interments,

leaving no room for more burials. Since that time the cemetery has been closed to additional interments except for cremated remains or a casket burial in the same gravesite of a family member.

Since 1975 the San Antonio National Cemetery has been under the Fort Sam Houston National Cemetery for management and administration. On November 22, 1999, the cemetery was accepted for listing in the National Register of Historic Places.

Notable Persons

Buffalo Soldiers

There are 281 identified Buffalo Soldiers in the cemetery. These African Americans, named Buffalo Soldiers by their Native American opponents because of their hair and bravery, served in the 9th and 10th Cavalry and 24th and 25th Infantry Regiments on the frontier in the years following the Civil War. These black soldiers were often the only protection for the white settlers against the Indians.

Pershing's Chinese

Twelve Chinese civilian employees of the US Army Quartermaster Corps are buried in Section H. Five of these are also listed as "refugees." The first Chinese immigrants to Texas arrived in 1870–1871 from California, where they had worked on building railroads. Their population in the state increased to over 800 before the Chinese Exclusion Act of 1882—enacted to preserve jobs for white residents—ended further immigration.

After the Exclusion Act a few hundred Chinese immigrated to northern Mexico where they intermarried with the natives and established general stores. Mexican officials were not happy with their success and targeted them for racially motivated violence. Many of the Chinese were killed; others crossed illegally into Texas or returned to China, while still others reduced their profile and remained in Mexico.

There was other unrest in Mexico at the time, with revolutionists, counterrevolutionists, and out-and-out banditry common. On March 9, 1916, paramilitary forces led by Pancho Villa crossed the border and raided the town of Columbus, New Mexico, killing eighteen soldiers and citizens and destroying buildings and property. The United States responded by ordering Major

Gen. John J. Pershing to lead an expedition of nearly 7,000 soldiers across the border to pursue and capture Villa and his men.

Pershing's army was not logistically prepared for the extended operations of what became known as the Mexican Punitive Expedition. The army's Quartermaster Services were neither sufficiently manned nor financed to support such a mission. Pershing's army prepared to "live off the land," and they soon found allies in their supply efforts. Chinese merchants on the Texas side joined the army with their supply wagons and were reinforced by Chinese in Mexico once they crossed the border. For the remainder of the operation, the Chinese provided what became the army's first mobile exchanges as they offered cooking and washing services. More importantly, they provided "comfort supplies," including tobacco, matches, candy, fruit, and soap.

The Punitive Expedition killed several of Villa's subordinates and soldiers but failed to capture the bandit himself. With the rising threat of World War I and pressure from the sitting Mexican government, Pershing began withdrawing back to Texas in early 1917. Aware that the Chinese who had supported his army would be severely punished or killed by one or the other of the Mexican opposing forces for their support of the Americans, Pershing sought and got permission to bring his Chinese helpers back across the border with him. By June, more than 400 Chinese had arrived in the vicinity of San Antonio. Many went to work for the Quartermaster Corps for twenty cents per hour to clear the land and build what became Camp Travis and other military sites that were being established to support the mobilization for World War I. Others worked in laundries and mess halls at Fort Sam Houston.

Pershing did not forget "his Chinese." When he returned from leading the American Expeditionary Force in Europe in 1919 as the General of the Armies—the highest rank ever bestowed on any American officer at the time—he began a campaign to secure legal permanent resident status for his Chinese. On November 23, 1921, President Warren G. Harding signed Public Law 29, granting Pershing's Chinese residency rights.

Twelve of Pershing's Chinese, employees of the Quartermaster Corps, are buried in Section H. Their standard military headstones contain their name and the notations "Q.M.C. employee." On May 27, 2011, a marker to the Chinese was dedicated at 2998 Wilson Way on Fort Sam Houston. Several of the offspring of Pershing's refugees who are still a part of the San Antonio Chinese community were in attendance.

Maj. Placidus Ord

Placidus Ord gains notable status by birth rather than personal accomplishments. Born on Christmas Day, 1821, in the District of Columbia, Ord attended Georgetown University and served in the Union Army, including time on the staff of Gen. William T. Sherman, during the Civil War. He remained in the army following the war and was posted to San Antonio, where he died in a carriage accident on July 9, 1876.

According to family stories and documents now in the Georgetown University Library, Ord was a descendant of King George IV of Great Britain. His father James was adopted in England shortly after his birth by Mr. and Mrs. James Ord and taken to the United States. There is strong evidence in the library's records that the senior James was the illegitimate son of George Augustus Frederick (the future King George IV) and his companion, Maria F. Fitzherbert. (Section A, Grave 105)

Capt. Orsemus Bronson Boyd

Orsemus Bronson Boyd was the principal speaker at the San Antonio National Cemetery on Decoration Day (later renamed Memorial Day), May 30, 1885. Born in 1844 in Croton, New York, Boyd enlisted in the 89th Regiment of New York Volunteers with his brother and father at the outbreak of the Civil War. In 1863, Boyd entered the US Military Academy, where he graduated as a second lieutenant in the cavalry in 1867. A year later he was promoted to first lieutenant. He remained in that rank for the next fourteen years as he served in Texas and the Southwest in operations against the Native Americans.

Boyd's career was fairly typical of the times, with slow promotions and difficult, hazardous duty. His burial place would not be all that remarkable except that a mere seven weeks after his Decoration Day speech he died of illness while in pursuit of the Apache leader Geronimo near Grafton, New Mexico, on July 23, 1885. His remains were returned to and interred in the same cemetery where he had recently spoken. (Section A, Grave 102)

Brig. Gen. John L. Bullis

John L. Bullis served with distinction in the Civil War, the Indian Wars, and the Spanish American War. A native of Macedon, New York, he enlisted as a private in the 126th New York Volunteer Infantry early in the Civil War, only to be captured at the Battle of Harpers Ferry in 1862. After a prisoner exchange, he rejoined the infantry and was wounded and again captured at the Battle of Gettysburg the following year. After another prisoner exchange, he secured a commission as a captain in the 118th US Colored Troops, primarily composed of former slaves.

After the war he briefly returned to civilian life before rejoining the army in 1867 as a second lieutenant in the 41st and later the 24th Infantry—both black units. In 1873, Bullis reported to Fort Clark, Texas, where he assumed command of the Seminole Indian Scouts. Over the next decade he served under Gen. Ranald S. Mackenzie in operations primarily against the Apaches. The Texas Legislature presented him a "special thanks" with a resolution on April 7, 1882, for his efforts against the Indians. He then assumed the duties of Indian agent to the Pueblo and Apache tribes in New Mexico. In 1897 he became the paymaster of Fort Sam Houston in San Antonio before joining the US expedition to Cuba in the Spanish American War.

Bullis was promoted to brigadier general shortly before his retirement in 1905 in San Antonio. He died of a stroke while watching a boxing match on the post on May 26, 1911. He is buried with his second wife and a daughter. When the US Army began its expansion for World War I, it opened a large training base north of San Antonio and named it Camp Bullis in his honor. (Section A, Grave 174)

2nd Lt. George E.M. Kelly

Born in London, England, George E.M. Kelly immigrated to America and joined the US Army in 1904. After a tour in the infantry, he volunteered for the Aeronautical Division of the US Signal Corps and became one of the army's first pilots. On May 10, 1911, he died in an air crash at Fort Sam Houston—the second army aviator to die while piloting an airplane. Camp Kelly, southwest of San Antonio, later Kelly Air Force Base, was named in his honor when it opened in 1917. (Section A, Grave 117A)

Gustav Schleicher

The largest private monument in the San Antonio National Cemetery, or in any other Texas VA burial ground, stands above the grave of a man who never wore the uniform of any of the US Armed Forces. Gustav Schleicher, born in 1823, emigrated from Germany to Texas in 1847 as a part of a communist commune established on the banks of the Llano River. He soon found the communist community had few merits and wrote, "The bigger the men, the more they talked, the less they worked and the more they ate." The community failed within a year, but Schleicher had already departed to embrace capitalism.

He established a shingle mill near New Braunfels and in 1850 moved to San Antonio, where he began building bridges and railroads—including a route from the city to Port Lavaca. In 1852 he secured his American citizenship and then served for two years in the Texas Legislature. From 1854 to 1861 he acted as the surveyor of the Bexar County Land District.

Schleicher opposed the formation of the Confederate States of America, but when Texas seceded, he joined the Southern army as a captain of engineers under Gen. John B. Magruder. He returned to San Antonio after the war and resumed his railroad building and political career. In 1874 he was elected to the US House of Representatives. He died on January 10, 1879. His friends and business associates arranged for his burial in the veterans cemetery and financed the tall marble obelisk that stands above his grave and dominates the cemetery's skyline. Schleicher County in far West Texas is named in his honor. (Section A, Grave 140)

Medal of Honor Recipients

The San Antonio National Cemetery is the last resting place for fourteen veterans who earned the Medal of Honor during the Civil War, Indian Wars, Spanish American War, and World War I. Their backgrounds, stories, and the "firsts" that they established are some of the most interesting of any national cemetery.

Pvt. Simon Suhler
(Simon Neustadle, Charles Gardner)

The most unusual Medal of Honor recipient's grave in the San Antonio cemetery—and for that matter, in any Texas or other national VA cemetery—is that of Simon Suhler. Born in Bavaria, Germany, in 1844, Suhler immigrated to the United States sometime before the Civil War and, shortly after the outbreak of hostilities, joined the 32nd Indiana Regiment, a unit made up primarily of ethnic Germans and led by a former Prussian officer.

Suhler was wounded and captured at the Battle of Shiloh in 1862. After a prisoner exchange, he returned to his unit but soon deserted. He then joined the 11th Heavy Artillery and later the 4th New York Heavy Artillery under the name of Simon Neustadle and served honorably for the remainder of the conflict. After a brief time as a civilian, Suhler again enlisted in the US Army and joined the 8th Cavalry Regiment under the name of Charles Gardner.

In the summer and fall of 1868, Gardner and his fellow troopers of the 8th Cavalry pursued bands of Apaches who were killing settlers and stealing livestock in Arizona Territory. The following summer he was presented the Medal of Honor in a simple citation that states he was cited for "Bravery in scouts and actions against the Indians." He is one of twenty-seven Jewish Americans to receive the medal.

Gardner left the 8th Cavalry after twelve years of service and took up residence in San Antonio. Upon his death in 1895, he was buried under a headstone with his assumed name. It was not until more than ninety years later that his family came forward with proof of his actual identity. On Veterans Day, 1988, a corrected headstone was place on Suhler's grave. (Section I, Grave 1610)

Pvt. William H. Barnes

Born into slavery in Maryland in 1840 or 1841, William H. Barnes joined the 38th United States Colored Infantry in 1864 and participated in the Battle of Chaffin's Farm, Virginia, on September 29 of that year. In an attack against defenses held by Gen. John Gregg's Texas Brigade, nearly half of Barnes's regiment were killed, wounded, or captured. On the following April 6, Barnes shared orders with eleven other black soldiers awarding them Medals of Honor for their actions in the battle. These were the first African Americans so honored. The list was alphabetical, with Barnes at the top of the list, making him the first black Medal of Honor recipient. His citation simply states that he was "among the first to enter the enemy's works, although wounded."

Barnes, now a sergeant, remained with his regiment after the war when it moved to Texas on occupation duty. There in 1866 he contacted tuberculosis and died in an army hospital near Indianola on December 24. His wooden grave marker was lost to the elements before all of the remains from this cemetery were moved to San Antonio after the post closed, and so his remains are among those buried in a common grave in Section H. A separate memorial marker was later placed in his honor. (Section MA, Site 86)

Cpl. John J. Given, Sgt. William DeArmond, Pvt. George W. Smith

Along with Barnes's marker in Section MA, there are similar memorials to three other recipients of the Medal of Honor whose exact burial places are unknown.

Born in Kentucky, John J. Given enlisted in the 6th US Cavalry Regiment in 1866. Four years later he was stationed at Fort Richardson, Texas, where he joined a patrol of three officers and fifty-three enlisted men in pursuit of Comanche Indians who had attacked a mail stage wagon at Rock Springs. By the time they caught up with the marauders on July 12 on the Middle Fork of the Little Wichita River, the Indian band had grown to more than 250 warriors. The cavalrymen took up defensive positions and, in a four-hour fight, forced the Indians to retreat. During the battle, Given went to the aid of a wounded friend and was killed by Kicking Bird, the Kiowa chief, who rode out of an arroyo and drove his war lance into the soldier's back, killing him instantly. Given's body was captured by the Indians and never recovered. A general order from Commander, Department of Texas, stated, "This engagement doubtless saved the frontier counties of Northwest Texas from a most destructive raid from 250 Indians." A memorial marker honors his service. (Section MA, Site 88)

DeArmond joined the 5th US Infantry Regiment from his home in Ohio in 1866. On September 9, 1874, while escorting a supply train from Fort Supply, Indian Territory, to Texas, his unit was attacked by a vastly superior number of Comanche and Kiowa warriors. The infantrymen managed to hold off the Indians despite repeated attacks over the next three days before reinforcement arrived. During the battle DeArmond was killed, and his body fell into the hands of the Indians and was never recovered. His Medal of Honor citation reads, "For gallantry in action." His memorial stone is in Section MA, Site 89.

George W. Smith, a native of New York, was a member of the 6th US Cavalry that engaged a large force of Comanche and Kiowa Indians in an area between Gageby Creek and the Wichita River in Texas. In what became known as the Buffalo Wallow Fight, Smith and five other cavalrymen turned back attack after attack by the Indians on September 12, 1874. Although wounded early in the battle, Smith continued to fight until shot again in the chest. Col. Nelson Miles, his regimental commander, later wrote of Smith and his fellow troopers, "The simple recital of their deeds and the mention of the odds against which they fought; how the wounded defended the dying, and the dying aided the wounded by exposure to fresh wounds after the power of action was gone, these alone present a scene of cool courage, heroism, and self-sacrifice, which duty as well as inclination prompt us to recognize, but which we cannot fitly honor."

Smith's fellow cavalrymen buried him near where he fell. The exact gravesite has been lost over time. A Texas Historical Marker stands near the battle site, and a memorial headstone is in Section MA, Site 87.

Sgt. James Howard

A native of New Jersey, James Howard joined the 158th New York Infantry and earned his Medal of Honor during an attack against Battery Gregg in the Battle of Petersburg, Virginia, on

April 2, 1865. His citation states that he "carried the colors in advance of the line of battle, the flagstaff being shot off while he was planting in on the parapet of the fort." Howard survived the war and moved to Texas, where he died on November 9, 1879. (Section E, Grave 889)

Sgt. Henry Falcott

Born in France in 1835, Henry Falcott immigrated to the United States and joined the US Army in San Francisco. As a trooper in the 8th US Cavalry Regiment, Falcott engaged hostile Apaches in Arizona Territory between August and October 1868. The following summer, Falcott and thirty-three other members of his regiment each received the Medal of Honor for "bravery in scouts and actions against Indians" on July 24, 1869. It was the largest number of Medal of Honor presentations at the time. Falcott rose to the rank of first sergeant before retiring and moving to Texas. He died there on December 2, 1910, at age seventy-five. (Section F, Grave 918)

Pvt. Solon D. Neal

Solon D. Neal, a New Hampshire native, earned his medal in a fight against Comanche and Kiowa Indians on July 12, 1870, on the Wichita River of Texas with the 6th Cavalry Regiment. His citation reads, "For gallantry in action." Upon his retirement, he settled in San Antonio at 109 Wyoming Street—the current location of HemisFair '68's Tower of the Americas. Neal died on November 20, 1920. (Section G, Grave 1323)

Cpl. Henry A. McMasters

Born in Maine, Henry A. McMasters joined the 4th Cavalry Regiment and earned his medal for "gallantry in action" against Comanche Indians in the Battle of Red River in Texas on September 29, 1872. McMasters survived the fight but died a short time later on November 11 of unknown causes. (Section D, Grave 729)

Pvt. John Harrington

John Harrington, a Michigan native, earned his medal in the same battle where George W. Smith died on the Wichita River of Texas on September 12, 1874, with the 6th Cavalry Regiment. He served for more than twenty addition years before retiring to San Antonio, where he died on January 3, 1905. His citation states, "While carrying dispatches was attacked by 125 hostile Indians, whom he and his comrades fought throughout the day. He was severely wounded in the hip and unable to move. He continued to fight, defending an exposed dying man." (Section F, Grave 1012)

1st Lt. Lewis Warrington III

Born in Washington, DC, on an unknown date, Lewis Warrington III was the grandson of the War of 1812 naval hero Comm. Lewis Warrington. The younger Warrington joined the 4th Cavalry Regiment and led a small patrol against Comanche Indians at Muchague Valley, Texas, on December 8, 1874. In the pursuit that ended with hand-to-hand combat, Warrington killed or captured all but one of the hostiles. His citation states that he was awarded the medal "for gallantry in combat with five Indians." He died on January 5, 1879. (Section A, Grave 60)

Pvt. Frederick Deetline

German-born Frederick Deetline earned his medal in one of the US Cavalry's most famous battles. As the blacksmith for Company D, 7th Cavalry Regiment, Deetline participated in the Battle of the Little Big Horn in Montana against Sioux warriors and their allies on June 25, 1876. Deetline was with one of the supporting columns and did not die with George Custer's detachment. His citation states that he was decorated because he "voluntarily brought water to the wounded under fire." He died on December 3, 1910, in San Antonio. (Section G, Grave 921)

Pvt. James J. Nash

A Spanish-American War recipient of the Medal of Honor also lies in the San Antonio cemetery. James J. Nash of Kentucky, as a member of the 10th Infantry Regiment, earned the award when he "gallantly assisted in the rescue of wounded from in front of the lines and under heavy fire from the enemy" at Santiago, Cuba, on July 1, 1898. He died on June 11, 1927. (Section T, Grave 1461-A)

Pvt. David B. Barkley

David B. Barkley was born in Laredo, Texas, in 1899 to Antonia Cantu, a Mexican mother, and Josef Barkley, an American soldier from Pennsylvania. Barkley's family moved to San Antonio in 1904. At the outbreak of World War I, Barkley joined the Texas Guard and trained at Camps Travis and Bowie before joining the 89th Infantry Division in France, where he participated in the action in the Argonne near Pouilly-sur-Meuse during the war's final days.

On November 9, 1918, two days before the war ended, Barkley and another soldier volunteered to swim across the icy Meuse River to reconnoiter enemy positions. They penetrated 400 meters behind the German lines and then attempted to recross the river. Barkley drowned in the cold waters, but his companion made it back with the much-needed intelligence. Barkley's citation states, "When information was desired as to the enemy's position on the opposite side of the Meuse River, Pvt. Barkley, with another soldier, volunteered without hesitation and swam the river to reconnoiter the exact location. He succeeded in reaching the opposite bank, despite the evident determination of the enemy to prevent a crossing. Having obtained his information, he again entered the water for his return, but before his goal was reached, he was seized with cramps and drowned."

Barkley's heroism was the war's last such act to be recognized with the Medal of Honor. He was buried in France, but, at the request of his mother, his remains were returned to San Antonio in 1921. His body was met by an honor guard, and his casket lay in state first at his mother's home on Belvin Street, then at the Alamo, and finally at the San Fernando Cathedral before burial. In addition to being the last recipient of the medal in World War I, Barkley is the first Texas Hispanic American so decorated. Camp Barkeley (the misspelling apparently a clerical error that was never corrected), a training center for World War II soldiers near Abilene, Texas, was named in his honor. (Section G, Grave 1302)

Fort Sam Houston National Cemetery

San Antonio, Texas

San Antonio has been a center of military activity since before Texas became an independent nation and then a state. Several sites, including the Alamo, and camps in and around the city were used in deploying and supplying the expedition south in the Mexican War and against the Native American tribes on the frontier. It was not until 1876, however, that a permanent post was established and named the Post of San Antonio. It was renamed Fort Sam Houston in honor of the Texas general and politician on September 11, 1890.

For several decades Fort Sam, as it became known, buried its dead in the San Antonio National Cemetery until that designated area eventually filled up and became surrounded by the city's cemeteries. Post officials had to look for new land and, in 1924,

MAP OF THE

FORT SAM HOUSTON NATIONAL CEMETERY

1520 HARRY WURZBACH ROAD, SAN ANTONIO, TEXAS 78209

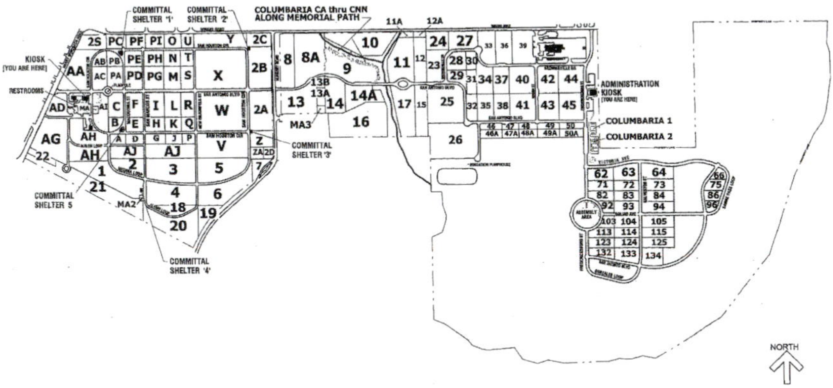

found it by setting aside a portion of Fort Sam as the post cemetery. The first interment was made two years later. About this same time, cemetery caretakers planted live oak trees alongside Sam Houston Drive in what is now in the northwestern portion of the cemetery. Today the trees' overhanging branches make for one of the most beautiful and serene vistas in any national cemetery.

On August 6, 1931, the US War Department transferred 60 acres, including the current graveyard, to the control of the San Antonio National Cemetery. In 1937 the War Department declared the cemetery independent and renamed it the Fort Sam Houston National Cemetery. Since that time the cemetery has grown to 338 acres to accommodate both casketed and cremated remains. With about 3,900 interments annually, the cemetery is the eighth most active national cemetery in the country.

Fort Sam Houston National Cemetery is the only facility in Texas with access to a horse-drawn caisson for funerals of sergeant majors and officers. The vehicle does not belong to the cemetery itself; rather, the wagon is owned and managed by adjacent Fort Sam Houston, which also maintains an honor guard of regular army soldiers for burial honors.

By the end of 2016, more than 150,000 veterans and their family members had been buried in the cemetery. A great variety of veterans make up this number, including nearly 400 general officers, 37 Buffalo Soldiers, 4 British Royal Air Force members, enemy POWs, and 13 recipients of the Medal of Honor.

Notable Groups

Buffalo Soldiers

Twenty-seven African American soldiers—veterans of the 9th and 10th Cavalry and the 24th and 25th Infantry Regiments—lie in Section PE. These soldiers were originally buried at frontier posts—including Forts Ringgold, McIntosh, Brown, Duncan, and Clark—before being reinterred at Fort Sam in 1947 when these remote installations closed following World War II.

Houston Riot and Courts Martial

When the Third Battalion of the 24th Infantry Regiment arrived in Houston's Camp Logan, a post located on the western edge of the city's downtown in what is now Memorial Park, the black soldiers found themselves welcomed by neither the citizens of the city nor its police force. After several incidents of unwarranted police brutality, the African Americans took matters into their own hands when they learned of a particularly brutal beating of one of their ranks by the Houston police. In the early evening of August 23, 1917, about 100 black soldiers shouldered their Springfield rifles and marched into the city. Two hours later, fifteen whites, including four police officers, lay dead with another twelve wounded. One of the wounded, a police officer, later died of his wounds. Five black soldiers were killed in the fight—the only racially motivated riot in US history where more whites than blacks were killed.

Over the next four months, 118 of the 24th Infantry soldiers were brought to court martial. Most were sentenced to long prison sentences. Thirteen were sentenced to hang. They were executed—on newly constructed scaffolding—on the banks of Salado Creek south of Fort Sam Houston before dawn on December 11, 1917. Six more were executed in September 1918. All nineteen were buried near where they died. In May 1937, seventeen of the soldiers' remains were removed and reinterred in Section PA, Graves 20–36. Their headstones, containing only their names and dates of death, make no mention of their unit, the riot, or their executions. The other two soldiers were reinterred in family plots.

Prisoners of War

In Section ZA along the cemetery's southwestern border are the graves of 140 POWs—132 Germans, 4 Italians, 3 Japanese, and 1 Austrian—who died in the United States during their captivity. These prisoners were reinterred in 1947 in the cemetery from various POW camps in Texas and Louisiana. Originally, the POWs were reburied in an isolated part of the cemetery, but over the years the area has been surrounded by other interments. The POWs' headstones are exactly like those of their former enemies who now surround their graves. The only difference is the notation of their country of service. Interestingly, two of the German graves have an etching of the Iron Cross, complete with the swastika symbol of Adolph Hitler's Nazi Party.

Group Burials

Before the development of DNA analysis and other forensic tests, it was often not possible to identify individuals who died in mass accidents or catastrophic combat. Many of these group casualties are buried in common graves under a single headstone bearing the name, rank, and date of death of each of the dead. The Fort Sam cemetery has ten of these group burial sites containing the remains of forty-eight veterans, with the largest containing ten airmen.

Notable Individuals

Capt. William M. Randolph (1893–1928)

William M. Randolph, an Austin native and graduate of Texas A&M, was killed when his AT-4 crashed at Gorman Field, Texas, on February 17, 1928. Randolph Field near San Antonio is named in his honor. At the time of his death, Randolph was on the selection committee seeking a name for the airfield. (Section Q, Grave 133)

Col. Charlie A. Beckwith (1929–1994)

Georgia-born Charlie A. Beckwith was the creator and first commander of the US Army's 1st Special Forces Operations Detachment, better known as Delta Force. (Section 9, Grave 1132)

Col. Felix A. "Doc" Blanchard (1924–2009)

A South Carolina native and veteran of World War II, Korea, and Vietnam, Felix A. "Doc" Blanchard won the NCAA football Heisman Trophy while playing at the US Military Academy in 1945. (Section 50, Grave 288)

Maj. Gen. Mary E. Clarke (1924–2011)

Mary E. Clark, born in New York, assumed command of the US Woman's Army Corps in 1975. She is the first woman to earn the rank of major general. (Section 50A, Grave 127)

Gustavo "Gus" C. Garcia (1915–1964)

Gustavo "Gus" C. Garcia, born in Laredo and raised in San Antonio, graduated from the University of Texas and served as a first lieutenant in the Pacific during World War II. He later became a civil rights attorney and argued Hernandez v. Texas before the US Supreme Court, a case in which the court ruled that US citizens could not be excluded from jury duty based on national origin. (Section V, Grave 2050)

Sgt. Maj. of the Army Leon Van Autreve (1920–2002)

Leon Van Autreve, born in Belgium, served as the Sergeant Major of the Army, the highest enlisted position, from 1973 to 1975. (Section A1, Grave 546)

Lt. Col. Robert Gottschall (1915–2005)

Dallas-native Robert Gottschall worked in Hollywood before being drafted into the army in World War II. Under the name of Robert Shaw, he made movies that include *The Grapes of Wrath* with Henry Fonda and *Adam Had Four Sons* with Ingrid Bergman and Susan Hayward as well as other feature films and multi-episode serials. After a brief return to Hollywood after the war, Gottschall went back on active duty and later retired to Texas. (Columbaria CAA-61)

Lt. Col. Karen Wagner (1961–2001)

A native of Houston, Karen Wagner played basketball at the University of Nevada at Las Vegas, where she earned a commission in the US Army through ROTC. Wagner died when radical Muslim terrorist crashed American Airlines Flight 77 into the Pentagon on September 11, 2001, killing all 64 aboard and 125 in the building. (Section 14, 1396)

Medal of Honor

Fireman 1st Cl. Peter Johnson

Born in England, Peter Johnson was aboard the USS *Vixen* during the Spanish-American War on the night of May 28, 1898. According to his citation, "Following the explosion of lower front manhole gasket of boiler A of the vessel Johnson displayed great coolness and self-possession in entering the fireroom." (Section F, Grave 442)

Col. Seth Lathrop Weld

The Maryland-born Seth Lathrop Weld earned his medal in the Philippine Insurrection while serving with the 8th Infantry Regiment on October 5, 1906, at La Paz, Leyte. According to his citation, "With his right arm cut open with a bolo, went to the assistance of a wounded constabulary officer and a fellow soldier who were surrounded by about 40 Pulajanes, and, using his disabled rifle as a club, beat back the assailants and rescued his party." (Section AH, Grave 189)

2nd Lt. Lloyd H. Hughes

Lloyd H. Hughes was a member of the Class of 1943 at Texas A&M University before leaving school to join the military a few weeks after the attack on Pearl Harbor. The citation for this airman in the 9th Air Force reads:

> On August 1, 1943, 2d Lt. Hughes served in the capacity of pilot of a heavy bombardment aircraft participating in a long and hazardous minimum-altitude attack against the Axis oil refineries of Ploesti, Rumania, launched from the northern shores of Africa. Flying in the last formation to attack the target, he arrived in the target area after previous flights had thoroughly alerted the enemy defenses. Approaching the target through intense and accurate antiaircraft fire and dense balloon barrages at dangerously low altitude, his plane received several direct hits from both large and small caliber antiaircraft guns which seriously damaged his aircraft, causing sheets of escaping gasoline to stream from the bomb bay and from the left wing. This damage was inflicted at a time prior to reaching the target when 2d Lt. Hughes could have made a forced landing. The target area was blazing with burning oil tanks and damaged refinery installations from which flames leaped high above the bombing level of the formation. With full knowledge of the consequences of entering this blazing inferno when his airplane was profusely leaking gasoline, 2d Lt. Hughes, motivated only by his high conception of duty which called for the destruction of his assigned target at any cost, did not elect to make a forced landing or turn back from the attack. Instead, rather than jeopardize the formation and the success of the attack, he unhesitatingly entered the blazing area and dropped his bomb load with great precision. After successfully bombing the objective, his aircraft emerged from the conflagration with the left wing aflame. Only then did he attempt a forced landing, but because of the advanced stage of the fire enveloping his aircraft the plane crashed and was consumed.

(Section U, Grave 53)

Staff Sgt. William J. Bordelon

William J. Bordelon, a San Antonio native, was the first US Marine from Texas to be awarded the Medal of Honor during World War II. His citation states:

> For valorous and gallant conduct above and beyond the call of duty as a member of an Assault Engineer Platoon of the First Battalion, Eighteenth Marines, tactically attached to the Second Marines, Second Marine Division, in action against the Japanese-held Atoll of Tarawa in the Gilbert Islands on November 20, 1943. Landing in the assault waves under withering enemy fire which killed all but four of the men in his tractor, Staff Sergeant Bordelon hurriedly made demolition charges and personally put two pill boxes out of action. Hit by enemy machine-gun fire just as a charge exploded in his hand while assaulting a third position, he courageously remained in action and, although out of demolition, provided himself with a rifle and furnished fire coverage for a group of men scaling the seawall. Disregarding his own serious condition, he unhesitatingly went to the aid of one of his demolition men, wounded and calling for help in the water, rescuing this man and another who had been hit by enemy fire while attempting to make the rescue. Still refusing first aid for himself, he again made up demolition charges and single-handedly assaulted a fourth Japanese machine-gun position but was instantly killed when caught in a final burst of fire from the enemy.

(Section Al, Grave 558)

Staff Sgt. Lucian Adams

Born into a Mexican American family in Port Arthur, Texas, Lucian Adams worked for two years building landing craft in a defense plant, the type of craft that he and his unit would later use in the invasions of Italy and France. He survived the war and died at age eighty in 2003. An elementary school on 9th Avenue in Port Arthur is named in his honor. He earned his medal near St. Die, France, on October 28, 1944, as a member of the 30th Infantry Regiment, 3rd Infantry Division. His citation states,

> When his company was stopped in its effort to drive through the Mortagne Forest to reopen the supply line to the isolated third battalion, S/Sgt. Adams braved the concentrated fire of machineguns in a lone assault on a force of German troops. Although his company had progressed less than 10 yards and had lost 3 killed and 6 wounded, S/Sgt. Adams charged forward dodging from tree to tree firing a borrowed BAR from the hip. Despite intense machinegun fire which the enemy directed at him and rifle grenades which struck the trees over his head

showering him with broken twigs and branches, S/Sgt. Adams made his way to within 10 yards of the closest machinegun and killed the gunner with a hand grenade. An enemy soldier threw hand grenades at him from a position only 10 yards distant; however, S/Sgt. Adams dispatched him with a single burst of BAR fire. Charging into the vortex of the enemy fire, he killed another machine gunner at 15 yards range with a hand grenade and forced the surrender of two supporting infantrymen. Although the remainder of the German group concentrated the full force of its automatic weapons fire in a desperate effort to knock him out, he proceeded through the woods to find and exterminate five more of the enemy. Finally, when the third German machinegun opened up on him at a range of 20 yards, S/Sgt. Adams killed the gunner with BAR fire. In the course of the action, he personally killed nine Germans, eliminated three enemy machineguns, vanquished a specialized force which was armed with automatic weapons and grenade launchers, cleared the woods of hostile elements, and reopened the severed supply lines to the assault companies of his battalion.

(Section A1, Grave 555)

Col. Cecil Hamilton Bolton

Florida-born Hamilton Bolton earned his medal as a first lieutenant with the 413th Infantry Regiment of the 104th Infantry Division near the Mark River in the Netherlands on November 2, 1944. He remained in the army after World War II and rose to the rank of colonel before his death in 1965. His citation states: "Bolton was wounded in the legs by a German artillery shell. Despite these wounds, he took two men and led them in a successful assault against three German positions which were firing on his company. Wounded a second time, he ordered his two companions to leave him behind and head for the safety of the American lines. He then crawled the rest of the way back to his company." (Section PC, Grave 22-J)

Sgt. Jose M. Lopez

Born and orphaned in Mexico, Jose M. Lopez moved to Mission, Texas, as a child. As a young man, he boxed professionally under the name of Kid Mendoza before joining the US Merchant Marines. After the attack on Pearl Harbor, he enlisted in the US Army and went ashore at Normandy. He remained in the army after the war, later served in Korea, and retired as a master sergeant. There is a statue, park, and street named in his honor in Mission and another statue in Brownsville. He died at age ninety-four in 2005.

On December 17, 1944, he was with the 23rd Infantry Regiment, 2nd Infantry Division near Krinkelt, Belgium, where he earned his Medal. His citation states:

> On his own initiative, he carried his heavy machinegun from Company K's right flank to its left, in order to protect that flank which was in danger of being overrun by advancing enemy infantry supported by tanks. Occupying a shallow hole offering no protection above his waist, he cut down a group of 10 Germans. Ignoring enemy fire from an advancing tank, he held his position and cut down 25 more enemy infantry attempting to turn his flank. Glancing to his right, he saw a large number of infantry swarming in from the front. Although dazed and shaken from enemy artillery fire which had crashed into the ground only a few yards away, he realized that his position soon would be outflanked. Again, alone, he carried his machinegun to a position to the right rear of the sector; enemy tanks and infantry were forcing a withdrawal. Blown over backward by the concussion of enemy fire, he immediately reset his gun and continued his fire. Single-handed he held off the German horde until he was satisfied his company had effected its retirement. Again he loaded his gun on his back and in a hail of small arms fire he ran to a point where a few of his comrades were attempting to set up another defense against the onrushing enemy. He fired from this position until his ammunition was exhausted. Still carrying his gun, he fell

> back with his small group to Krinkelt. Sgt. Lopez's gallantry and intrepidity, on seemingly suicidal missions in which he killed at least 100 of the enemy, were almost solely responsible for allowing Company K to avoid being enveloped, to withdraw successfully and to give other forces coming up in support time to build a line which repelled the enemy drive.

(Section A1, Grave 542)

Technical Sgt. Cleto Luna Rodriguez

Cleto Luna Rodriguez was born in San Marcos, Texas, and worked as a newspaper carrier selling papers in the famous Gunter Hotel in San Antonio until he enlisted in the US Army in 1944. He later served in the US Air Force before rejoining the army and retiring as a master sergeant in 1970. He died in 1990. An elementary school in San Antonio and a firing range at Camp Perry, Ohio, are named in his honor, as is an 8.5-mile stretch of Texas Highway 90 between Interstate 410 and Interstate 35.

Rodriguez received his medal as a member of the 148th Infantry Regiment, 37th Infantry Division for actions on February 9, 1945, at Paco Railroad Station, Manila, Philippine Islands. His citation states:

> Technical Sergeant Rodriguez was an automatic rifleman when his unit attacked the strongly defended Paco Railroad Station during the battle for Manila, Philippine Islands. While making a frontal assault across an open field, his platoon was halted 100 yards from the station by intense enemy fire. On his own initiative, he left the platoon, accompanied by a comrade, and continued forward to a house 60 yards from the objective. Although under constant enemy observation, the two men remained in this position for an hour, firing at targets of opportunity, killing more than 35 hostile soldiers and wounding many more. Moving closer to the station and discovering a group of Japanese replacements attempting to reach pillboxes, they opened heavy fire, killed more than 40 and stopped all subse-

> quent attempts to man the emplacements. Enemy fire became more intense as they advanced to within 20 yards of the station. Then, covered by his companion, Private Rodriguez boldly moved up to the building and threw five grenades through a doorway killing seven Japanese, destroying a 20-mm gun and wrecking a heavy machinegun. With their ammunition running low, the two men started to return to the American lines, alternately providing covering fire for each other's withdrawal. During this movement, Rodriguez' companion was killed. In 2½ hours of fierce fighting the intrepid team killed more than 82 Japanese, completely disorganized their defense, and paved the way for the subsequent overwhelming defeat of the enemy at this strongpoint. Two days later, Private Rodriguez again enabled his comrades to advance when he single-handedly killed six Japanese and destroyed a well-placed 20-mm gun by his outstanding skill with his weapons, gallant determination to destroy the enemy, and heroic courage in the face of tremendous odds, Rodriguez, on two occasions, materially aided the advance of our troops in Manila.

(Section A-1, Grave 700)

Platoon Sgt. William George Harrell

William George Harrell, born in Rio Grande City, Texas, enrolled in Texas A&M University as member of the Class of 1943. He left A&M in 1941 to work for funds to continue his education and then enlisted in the Marine Corps after the attack on Pearl Harbor. On February 19, 1945, he went ashore on Iwo Jima as a rifleman in the 28th Regiment of the 5th Marine Division. In a fight on March 2–3, Harrell earned his medal while losing his right hand to a grenade explosion. His left hand also had to be amputated later.

After the war Harrell was fitted with prosthetic hands and worked for the VA in San Antonio. On August 9, 1964, Harrell apparently killed two friends and then committed suicide. No motive was ever determined.

A monument of Harrell stands in the center of Mercedes, Texas, where he went to high school. There is also a middle school in the town named for him. Texas A&M named a dormitory in his honor, and his medal is on permanent display in the university's Sam Houston Sanders Corps of Cadets Center.

His citation states:

> Standing watch alternately with another Marine in a terrain studded with caves and ravines, Sergeant Harrell was holding a position in a perimeter defense around the company command post when Japanese troops infiltrated our lines in the early hours of dawn. Awakened by a sudden attack, he quickly opened fire with his carbine and killed two of the enemy as they emerged from a ravine in the light of a star-shell burst. Unmindful of his danger as hostile grenades fell closer, he waged a fierce lone battle until an exploding missile tore off his left hand and fractured his thigh; he was attempting to reload the carbine when his companion returned from the command post with another weapon. Wounded again by a Japanese who rushed the foxhole wielding a saber in the darkness, Sergeant Harrell succeeded in drawing his pistol and killing his opponent and then ordered his wounded companion to a place of safety. Exhausted by profuse bleeding but still unbeaten, he fearlessly met the challenge of two more enemy troops who charged his position and placed a grenade near his head. Killing one man with his pistol, he grasped the sputtering grenade with his good right hand and, pushing it painfully toward the crouching soldier, saw his remaining assailant destroyed but his own hand severed in the explosion. At dawn Sergeant Harrell was evacuated from a position hedged by the bodies of twelve dead Japanese, at least five of whom he had personally destroyed in his self-sacrificing defense of the command post.

(Section W, Grave 3247)

1st Lt. James E. Robinson Jr.

Born in Ohio, James E. Robinson entered the army at Waco, Texas. He earned his medal on April 6, 1945, a month before the end of the war in Europe as an artillery forward observer in the 63rd Infantry Division. A navy transport ship (AKV3) was named in his honor. According to his citation:

> He was a field artillery forward observer attached to Company A, 253d Infantry, near Untergriesheim, Germany, on 6 April 1945. Eight hours of desperate fighting over open terrain swept by German machinegun, mortar, and small-arms fire had decimated Company A, robbing it of its commanding officer and most of its key enlisted personnel when 1st Lt. Robinson rallied the 23 remaining uninjured riflemen and a few walking wounded, and, while carrying his heavy radio for communication with American batteries, led them through intense fire in a charge against the objective. Ten German infantrymen in foxholes threatened to stop the assault, but the gallant leader killed them all at point-blank range with rifle and pistol fire and then pressed on with his men to sweep the area of all resistance. Soon afterward he was ordered to seize the defended town of Kressbach. He went to each of the 19 exhausted survivors with cheering words, instilling in them courage and fortitude, before leading the little band forward once more. In the advance he was seriously wounded in the throat by a shell fragment, but, despite great pain and loss of blood, he refused medical attention and continued the attack, directing supporting artillery fire even though he was mortally wounded. Only after the town had been taken and he could no longer speak did he leave the command he had inspired in victory and walk nearly 2 miles to an aid station where he died from his wound. By his intrepid leadership 1st Lt. Robinson was directly responsible for Company A's accomplishing its mission against tremendous odds.

(Section T, Grave 98)

Pfc. Milton Lee

Milton Lee was born in Louisiana and entered the army at San Antonio, Texas. He earned his medal as an infantryman in the 502nd Infantry Regiment of the 101st Airborne Division near Phu Bai, Republic of Vietnam, on April 26, 1968. Lee Gymnasium at Fort Campbell, Kentucky, is named in his honor. His citation states:

> Pfc. Lee was serving as the radio telephone operator with the 3d platoon, Company B. As lead element for the company, the 3d platoon received intense surprise hostile fire from a force of North Vietnamese Army regulars in well-concealed bunkers. With 50 percent casualties, the platoon maneuvered to a position of cover to treat their wounded and reorganize, while Pfc. Lee moved through the heavy enemy fire giving lifesaving first aid to his wounded comrades. During the subsequent assault on the enemy defensive positions, Pfc. Lee continuously kept close radio contact with the company commander, relaying precise and understandable orders to his platoon leader. While advancing with the front rank toward the objective, Pfc. Lee observed four North Vietnamese soldiers with automatic weapons and a rocket launcher lying in wait for the lead element of the platoon. As the element moved forward, unaware of the concealed danger, Pfc. Lee immediately, and with utter disregard for his own personal safety, passed his radio to another soldier and charged through the murderous fire. Without hesitation he continued his assault, overrunning the enemy position, killing all

occupants and capturing four automatic weapons and a rocket launcher. Pfc. Lee continued his 1-man assault on the second position through a heavy barrage of enemy automatic weapons fire. Grievously wounded, he continued to press the attack, crawling forward into a firing position and delivering accurate covering fire to enable his platoon to maneuver and destroy the position. Not until the position was overrun did Pfc. Lee falter in his steady volume of fire and succumb to his wounds. Pfc. Lee's heroic actions saved the lives of the lead element and were instrumental in the destruction of the key position of the enemy defense.

(Section X, Grave 2475)

M. Sgt. Roy P. Benavidez

Born in Lindenau, Texas, Roy P. Benavidez was orphaned at age seven and raised by relatives in El Campo. He joined the military in 1952 and in 1965 went on his first tour to Vietnam, where he was severely wounded by a land mine. After a lengthy recovery, he returned to Vietnam as a member of the Studies and Observations Group (SOG) of the 5th Special Forces Group, where he earned his medal on May 2, 1968. Due to the lack of living witnesses, Benavidez was not awarded his medal until 1981 when a previously unknown survivor of the battle came forward.

When President Ronald Reagan presented the medal, he said, "If the story of his heroism were a movie script, you would not believe it." More than a dozen schools, parks, military buildings, and other public facilities across the country are named in his honor. His medal is now on display in the Ronald Reagan Presidential Library.

His citations states:

> On the morning of 2 May 1968, a 12-man Special Forces Reconnaissance Team was inserted by helicopters of the 240th Assault Helicopter Company in a dense jungle area west of Loc Ninh, Vietnam, to gather intelligence information about confirmed large-scale enemy activity. This area was controlled and routinely patrolled by the North Vietnamese Army. After a short period of time on the ground, the team met heavy enemy resistance, and requested emergency extraction. Three helicopters attempted extraction, but were unable to land due to intense enemy small arms and anti-aircraft fire.
>
> Sergeant Benavidez was at the Forward Operating Base in Loc Ninh monitoring the operation by radio when these helicopters, of the 240th Assault Helicopter Company, returned to off-load wounded crew members and to assess aircraft damage. Sergeant Benavidez voluntarily boarded a returning aircraft to assist in another extraction attempt. Realizing that all the team members were either dead or wounded and unable to move to the pickup zone, he directed the aircraft to a nearby clearing where he jumped from the hovering helicopter, and ran approximately 75 meters under withering small arms fire to the crippled team.
>
> Prior to reaching the team's position, he was wounded in his right leg, face, and head. Despite these painful injuries, he took charge, repositioning the team members and directing their fire to facilitate the landing of an extraction aircraft, and the loading of wounded and dead team members. He then threw smoke canisters to direct the aircraft to the team's position. Despite his severe wounds and under intense enemy fire, he carried and dragged half of the wounded team members to the awaiting aircraft. He then provided protective fire by running alongside the aircraft as it moved to pick up the remaining team members. As the enemy's fire intensified, he hurried to recover the body and classified documents on the dead team leader.

When he reached the leader's body, Sergeant Benavidez was severely wounded by small arms fire in the abdomen and grenade fragments in his back. At nearly the same moment, the aircraft pilot was mortally wounded, and his helicopter crashed. Although in extremely critical condition due to his multiple wounds, Sergeant Benavidez secured the classified documents and made his way back to the wreckage, where he aided the wounded out of the overturned aircraft, and gathered the stunned survivors into a defensive perimeter. Under increasing enemy automatic weapons and grenade fire, he moved around the perimeter distributing water and ammunition to his weary men, reinstilling in them a will to live and fight. Facing a buildup of enemy opposition with a beleaguered team, Sergeant Benavidez mustered his strength, began calling in tactical air strikes and directed the fire from supporting gunships to suppress the enemy's fire and so permit another extraction attempt.

He was wounded again in his thigh by small arms fire while administering first aid to a wounded team member just before another extraction helicopter was able to land. His indomitable spirit kept him going as he began to ferry his comrades to the craft. On his second trip with the wounded, he was clubbed from behind by an enemy soldier. In the ensuing hand-to-hand combat, he sustained additional wounds to his head and arms before killing his adversary. He then continued under devastating fire to carry the wounded to the helicopter. Upon reaching the aircraft, he spotted and killed two enemy soldiers who were rushing the craft from an angle that prevented the aircraft door gunner from firing upon them. With little strength remaining, he made one last trip to the perimeter to ensure that all classified material had been collected or destroyed, and to bring in the remaining wounded.

Only then, in extremely serious condition from numerous wounds and loss of blood, did he allow himself to be pulled into the extraction aircraft.

(Section A1, Grave 553)

C.W.O. 2 Louis R. Rocco

Born in Albuquerque, New Mexico, Louis R. Rocco joined the army in 1955 and served as an enlisted medic. On his second tour in Vietnam as a sergeant first class, he earned his medal near Katum, Republic of Vietnam, on May 24, 1970, as a part of Advisory Team 162, US Military Assistance Command. A youth center in San Antonio is named in his honor.

His citation states:

> WO (then sergeant first class) Rocco distinguished himself when he volunteered to accompany a medical evacuation team on an urgent mission to evacuate eight critically wounded Army of the Republic of Vietnam personnel. As the helicopter approached the landing zone, it became the target for intense enemy automatic weapons fire. Disregarding his own safety, WO Rocco identified and placed accurate suppressive fire on the enemy positions as the aircraft descended toward the landing zone. Sustaining major damage from the enemy fire, the aircraft was forced to crash land, causing WO Rocco to sustain a fractured wrist and hip and a severely bruised back. Ignoring his injuries, he extracted the survivors from the burning wreckage, sustaining burns to his own body. Despite intense

enemy fire, WO Rocco carried each unconscious man across approximately 20 meters of exposed terrain to the Army of the Republic of Vietnam perimeter. On each trip, his severely burned hands and broken wrist caused excruciating pain, but the lives of the unconscious crash survivors were more important than his personal discomfort, and he continued his rescue efforts. Once inside the friendly position, WO Rocco helped administer first aid to his wounded comrades until his wounds and burns caused him to collapse and lose consciousness. His bravery under fire and intense devotion to duty were directly responsible for saving three of his fellow soldiers from certain death. His unparalleled bravery in the face of enemy fire, his complete disregard for his own pain and injuries, and his performance were far above and beyond the call of duty and were in keeping with the highest traditions of self-sacrifice and courage of the military service.

(Section A1, Grave 549)

Kerrville National Cemetery

Kerrville, Texas

The Kerrville National Cemetery is the smallest veterans burial ground in Texas. Joshua David Brown, a veteran of the Texas Revolution and the US-Mexican War, settled the area that would become Kerrville in 1848. Brown and his wife, Sarah Jane Goss, owned 2,000 acres southeast of the city site where, in addition to farming and ranching, they established a family cemetery.

In 1919 the Benevolent War Risk Society began soliciting funds by popular subscription to build a hospital for the treatment of World War I veterans in the Kerrville area. The Schreiner family donated property along the Guadalupe River east of town to the society in April 1920. Construction of the hospital began later that year but in early 1921 ceased construction due to lack of funds. The Department of Texas of the American Legion then purchased

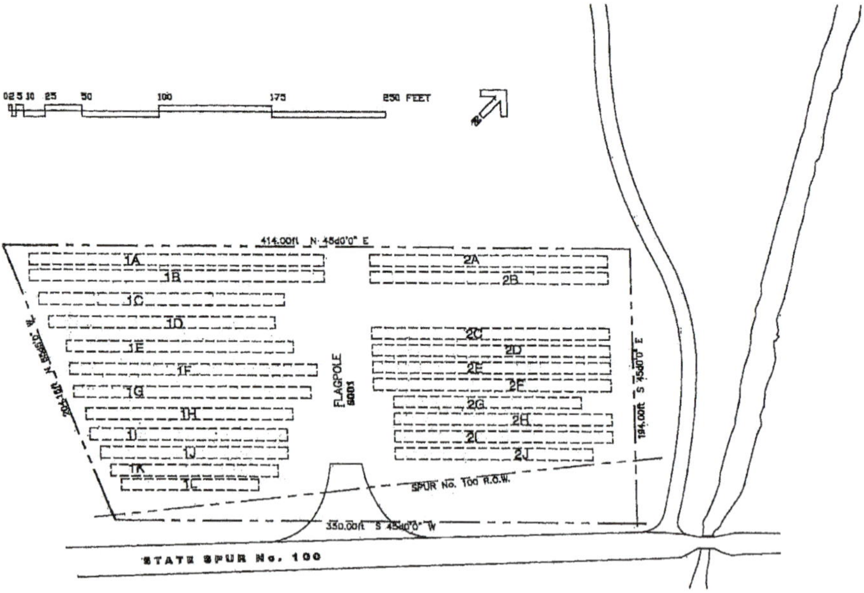

KERRVILLE NATIONAL CEMETERY

the property for one dollar and renewed soliciting funds for the hospital and grounds that became known as Legion.

In April 1921 the American Legion donated the unfinished hospital and its 748 acres to the State of Texas. The Texas Legislature appropriated $1.5 million to complete the hospital, and it opened and received its first patients on June 22 of that year. Initially the hospital focused on the care of tubercular patients and accepted veterans as well as those who were not. On June 1, 1923, the US Veterans Bureau (now the Department of Veterans Affairs) leased the complex from the state and opened it as a veterans care facility on July 12.

The US Veterans Bureau bought the hospital and its grounds in 1926 for $1,182,000. In 1952 it was renamed the Veterans Administration Hospital at Kerrville. Until that time the facility had always had “Legion” in its name, and many in Kerrville still refer to it by that name today. For its first four decades the hospital continued to focus on the treatment of veterans with tuberculosis but in 1960 expanded to become a general medical facility.

During the early years, many of the TB patients who did not survive were either indigent, without families, or otherwise had no one to pay for funeral costs or for transport to the VA cemeteries in San Antonio. In response, in 1923 descendants of Brown—A. P. Brown and J. S. Brown as trustees of the Brown-Doss Cemetery—gave the Women's Auxiliary of the Garrett-Baker Post of the American Legion permission to bury ex-servicemen who did not have anyone to provide burial expenses in the Kerrville area. In December 1932, the Brown Trust sold an additional part of the family cemetery to the Texas American Legion. At the same time the Garrett-Baker Women's Auxiliary relinquished its rights to the cemetery to the Texas Legion headquarters. The Texas American Legion donated the 1.7-acre cemetery, along

with its burial records, to the Veterans Administration in February 1943.

The first burial in what would become the Kerrville National Cemetery occurred on April 12, 1923—several months before the agreement between the Brown family and the Women's Auxiliary was actually reached. The last interment took place on October 28, 1957. That burial left no further space for additional burials, and the cemetery is now closed to future interments.

There is no welcome or information center at the cemetery. A nonelectronic kiosk at its main gate provides information and a map of the location of its 460 gravesites. Since 1973 the Fort Sam Houston National Cemetery has managed the facility.

Notable Interments

Spanish-American War Veterans

Many Texans, including those from the Kerrville area, volunteered to fight in the Spanish-American War of 1898. Several dozens of their graves are in the cemetery.

Clifford C. Hurlbert (unknown–1923)

Clifford C. Hurlbert, a Texas native, was interred on April 13, 1923—a day after his death at the Legion Hospital. He was the first to be buried in the cemetery. His stay and death at the hospital predated its takeover by the VA, and according to burial record notes published in a letter from the Department of the Army on December 27, 1957, Hurlbert had no active military service. (Section 1, Grave C-14)

James M. Brittain (1880–1957)

James M. Brittain, originally from Louisiana, was a veteran of World War I and achieved the rank of sergeant in the US Army. He is the last person to be interred in the cemetery with his burial on October 29, 1957. (Section 2, Grave A-18)

Fort Bliss National Cemetery

El Paso, Texas

Two mountain ranges dominate the area along the Rio Grande River where the country of Mexico and the states of Texas and New Mexico come together. From the time of the earliest Spanish explorers of the sixteenth century, this area has been known as El Paso del Norte (the Pass of the North). By the middle of the eighteen century, about 5,000 Spanish, mixed-bloods, and Indians had settled in the area. The Texas Revolution of 1836 and the US-Mexican War of 1846–1848 resulted in the land north of the Rio Grande becoming part of Texas and the United States.

FORT BLISS NATIONAL CEMETERY

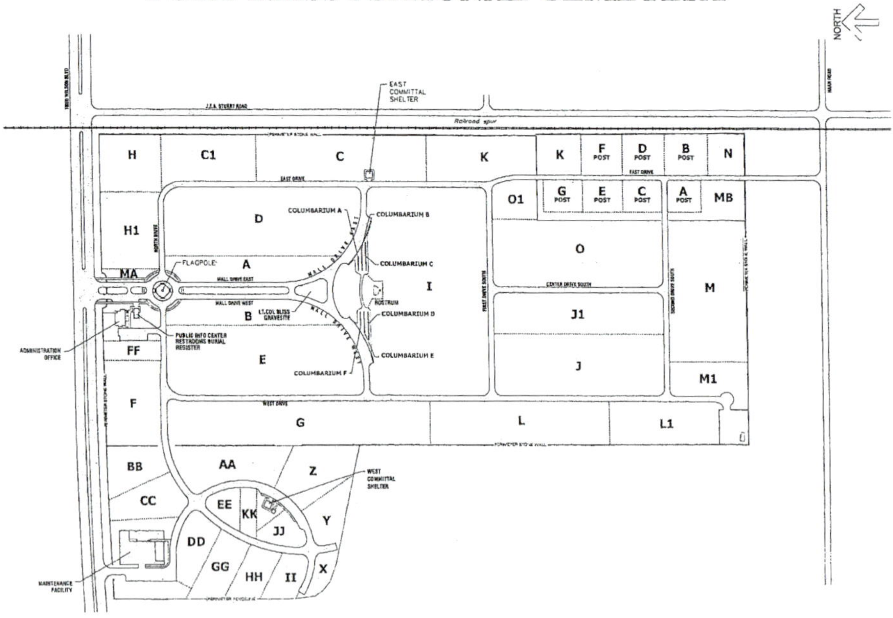

The expansion of the United States westward and the rush to the California gold fields in 1849 brought additional settlers and soldiers to what was then known as Franklin. Fort Bliss, named for Lt. Col. William S. Bliss, assistant adjutant general of the US Army, was established in 1854, and in 1859 the plat for the town of El Paso was completed, replacing Franklin. During the Civil War, Fort Bliss was occupied by Confederate forces and did not return to Union hands until the end of the conflict. The town on the south side of the river in Mexico remained El Paso del Norte, which caused confusion until it changed its name to Ciudad Juarez in 1888.

There are no definitive records dating establishment of the Fort Bliss cemetery, but apparently its first burial was in 1883. By 1890, the location contained 16 graves. In 1914, post officials set aside 2.2 acres, enclosed by a stone wall, with a capacity for an additional 800 interments. During the First World War, the cemetery more than doubled in size to reach a capacity for 2,400 burials.

Due to the increase in the veteran population as a result of World War I and the depleting burial space in existing facilities,

the US Congress passed a series of laws in 1936 that established seven new national cemeteries across the country. One of those was the new Fort Bliss National Cemetery, which included the old existing post burial ground. However, lack of funds and disagreements on the expansion area of the cemetery kept the Fort Bliss National Cemetery from opening until March 1939. The first interment took place a year later on March 7, 1940.

Today the Fort Bliss National Cemetery is still surrounded by a rock wall, but it has expanded to 82.1 acres. It contains the remains of more than 50,000 veterans' graves. One hundred or more burials are conducted monthly.

The Fort Bliss cemetery is one of only three national cemeteries that do not use traditional grass to cover its graves and grounds—the others being in Phoenix, Arizona, and Boulder City,

Nevada. El Paso and the surrounding area receive less than ten inches of rainfall per year, and water shortages are a constant threat. After much debate, the Fort Bliss cemetery converted from grass to become xeriscaped. Today fine stone gravel and native desert plants cover the graves and grounds. Along with becoming a national model on water conversation, the cemetery preserves the dignity and serenity worthy of the last resting place for America's veterans.

Notable Monuments

A monument dedicated to US Coast Guard and Navy personnel killed in the Japanese attack on Pearl Harbor on December 7, 1941, was dedicated in 1984. Monuments to military officers and to prisoners of war were erected in 1986.

Notable Interments

Lt. Col. William Wallace Smith Bliss (1815–1853)

New York–born William Wallace Smith Bliss graduated from West Point at age seventeen and was commissioned a second lieutenant in the infantry. A prodigy in most academic areas, he particularly excelled in mathematics and languages, being fluent in at least thirteen. His classmates so admired him that they nicknamed him "Perfect Bliss." He initially served in Alabama in 1833–1834 in operations to remove the Cherokees to the

Indian Territory. This was followed by four years as a math instructor back at West Point. During the Seminole War, he acted as the chief of staff to the commanding general from 1840 to 1841. After four years as a staff officer at a series of southern forts, he transferred to Texas, where he participated in the Mexican War, including the battles of Palo Alto, Resaca de la Palma, and Buena Vista.

Bliss served as chief of staff to Maj. Gen. Zachary Taylor during his entire time in Texas and Mexico. In 1848, Bliss married Taylor's youngest daughter, Mary Elizabeth, and accompanied the general to the White House as the president's private secretary after Taylor's election to the presidency that same year. President Taylor's wife took no part in social activities, and Mrs. Bliss essentially acted as first lady.

When Taylor died of an unknown digestive ailment in 1850, Bliss assumed the duties of adjutant-general of the Western Division of the Army. On a visit to New Orleans he contracted yellow fever and died on August 5, 1853. He was buried in the city's Girod Street Cemetery under a twenty-four-foot Italian marble memorial that noted he was "a finished scholar, an accomplished gentleman, and a gallant soldier." The following year, a new post was established near El Paso and named in his honor—although he was never assigned or even visited there.

In 1955 the City of New Orleans condemned the Girod Street Cemetery for the purpose of using the grounds for new roads and buildings in the business district. Remains of those interred there were removed to other cemeteries, and those of Lt. Col. Bliss were moved to the post and cemetery that bears his name. His grave, along the entrance driveway to the cemetery, is marked with a standard VA headstone. The marble memorial that marked his New Orleans grave was also moved to Fort Bliss and now stands near the installation's parade field.

Leo Robert Weismantel (1924–1961)

Native Texan Leo Robert Weismantel served as a medic with the 118th Coast Artillery Battalion in the US Army during World War II, attaining the rank of Tec 5. After his discharge, he pursued a film career under the name of Lee MacGregor and appeared in more than twenty-four films, including the role of Lieutenant Zimmerman in the 1949 Oscar-winning *Twelve O'clock High*. He retired from acting in 1952 and moved to El Paso, where he died in 1961. (Section D, Grave 1907)

John Markward Reynolds Jr. (1941–1966)

John Markward Reynolds earned the rank of specialist 4 in the US Army before becoming an actor after his discharge. As John Reynolds, he appeared in only one film—*The Hands of Fate*—which was produced in the El Paso area. A month before the film's release, Reynolds committed suicide. It was his only movie appearance. In recent years the film has reached cult status as one of the worst movies ever made. (Section D, Grave 2660)

Reece "Goose" Tatum (1921–1967)

Reece "Goose" Tatum, born and raised in Arkansas, played in the Negro Baseball League before joining the Harlem Globetrotters. Drafted in 1943, he served in the Army Air Corps at Lincoln Army Air Field, Nebraska, during World War II. After the war he rejoined the Globetrotters and became known as "the clown prince" of basketball, credited with inventing the hook shot. In 2011 he was inducted into the Naismith Memorial Basketball Hall of Fame. (Section D, Grave 2668)

Maj. Gen. Terry de la Mesa Allen Sr. (1888–1969) and Lt. Col. Terry de la Mesa Allen Jr. (1929–1967)

Terry de la Mesa Allen Sr. fought and was wounded in World War I as a captain. In World War II he commanded the 1st Infantry Division in North Africa and Sicily and then the 104th Infantry Division in France and Germany. Although highly regarded by his troops, he often had difficulties with his superiors. War correspondent Ernie Pyle wrote, "Major General Terry Allen was one of my favorite people. Partly because he didn't give a damn for hell or high water; partly because he was more colorful than most; and partly because he was the only general outside the Air Forces I could call by his first name. If there was one thing in the world Allen lived and breathed for, it was to fight. He had been all shot up in the last war, and he seemed not the least averse to getting shot again. This was no intellectual war with him. He hated Germans and Italians like vermin."

Allen Sr. retired from active duty shortly after the end of World War II and was active in business, civic affairs, and veterans groups in El Paso until his death. (Section A, Grave 196)

Terry de la Mesa Allen Jr. was killed in action on October 17, 1967, in a Viet Cong ambush near Lai Khe northwest of Saigon in the Battle of Ong Thanh while commanding the 2nd Battalion, 28th Infantry Regiment of his father's old 1st Infantry Division. An account of the battle and Allen Jr.'s death is detailed in David Maraniss's bestselling book *They Marched into Sunlight*. The book was later adapted into the PBS documentary *Two Days in October*. Allen Jr. and Allen Sr. rest side by side. (Section A, Grave 197)

Brig. Gen. S.L.A. Marshall (1900–1977)

S.L.A. Marshall, or SLAM, as he liked to be called, joined the army at age seventeen from his home in Catskill, New York, in 1917. He served as an enlisted man in Pershing's expedition against Pancho Villa and then as an engineer with the 90th Infantry Division in France during World War I. He secured an officer's commission while on occupation duty following the war before being discharged. Marshall joined the army reserves, attended the Texas College of Mines (now the University of Texas at El Paso), and worked as a newspaper reporter and editor in El Paso and Detroit. He gained a national reputation for his journalism in Latin America, Europe, and the Spanish Civil War.

Marshall advanced in rank in the reserves to brigadier general and went back on active duty during World War II as a combat historian. As one of the early proponents of oral history, he interviewed many of the war's best-known generals as well as hundreds of other officers and enlisted personnel. In his book about the war, *Men against Fire*, he claimed that 75 percent of combat soldiers never fired their weapons in battle. Although often quoted, there is no support for this claim, and it is dismissed today by veterans and historians alike.

Nevertheless, Marshall went on to write more than thirty books on World War II, the Korean War, and the Vietnam War. His book on Korea, *Pork Chop Hill: The American Fighting Man in Action,* was made into a popular movie by the same name. Although retired from the reserves, Marshall spent several months during 1966 and 1967 in Vietnam as the army chief of military history's representative. His escort in Vietnam was Col. David Hackworth, a highly decorated infantry veteran and a future military analysist for cable television. Hackworth later called Marshall a "voyeur warrior" for whom "the truth never got in the way of a good story." He added, "Veterans of many of the actions he 'documented' in his books have complained bitterly over the years of his inaccuracy or blatant bias." (Section A, Grave 124A)

[*Author's Note*: In Marshall's book *West to Cambodia,* he details operations by the 25th Infantry Division in Vietnam. He directly quotes my brother, Jim Lanning, who was an infantry platoon leader in the described operation. My brother states he was never interviewed by Marshall and never even met him.]

Sherman Alexander Hemsley (1938–2012)

Philadelphia-born Sherman Alexander Hemsley served in the US Air Force from 1954 to 1958, reaching the rank of airman third class. Hensley later starred in the longest-running television sitcom with a predominantly black cast from 1975 to 1985, an eleven-season run. As the costar of *The Jeffersons* on ABC Television, Hemsley garnered both Emmy and Golden Globe nominations. (Section M-1, Grave 73)

Sgt. Maj. of the Army (SMA) William O. Wooldridge (1922–2012)

Born in Oklahoma and raised in Texas, William O. Wooldridge earned two Silver Stars and a Purple Heart in the European Theater during World War II and participated in the Normandy D-Day Invasion. From 1966 to 1968, he served as the first sergeant major of the army—the highest enlisted rank in the service with responsibilities of advising and assisting the chief of staff of the US Army. Following his tour as SMA, Woodridge served in Vietnam as the sergeant major of the US Military Assistance Command, where he earned his second award of the Combat Infantryman Badge. He is the only SMA to ever hold that position and then return to field duty. (Section A, Grave 56)

Other Burials

In addition to US veterans and families, there are a number of non-US citizens buried at Fort Bliss, including allies and enemies. In 1944, China requested and was granted permission to bury in the cemetery their air force cadets who were killed in training in the El Paso area. By war's end fifty-five cadets were interred.

There are also four German prisoners of war buried in the cemetery as well as a German civilian scientist who had been conducting research at Fort Bliss. Three Japanese Americans, who died as civilian internees at a camp in Lordsburg, New Mexico, are also buried in the cemetery.

Medal of Honor Recipients

Pvt. George Hooker (1847–1873)

George Hooker joined Company K of 5th US Cavalry Regiment from his Maryland home and participated in Lt. Col. George Crook's operation to neutralize Western Apaches in Arizona's Tonto Basin. On January 22, 1873, Hooker was killed in a battle against the hostiles. His citation reads simply that his medal award was for "gallantry in action in which he was killed." His remains were not recovered. A memorial stone in his honor is in Section MA, Grave 30.

Cpl. Frank Brattling (1845–1873)

German-born Frank Brattling immigrated to the United States and entered the army in Louisville, Kentucky. In the summer of 1873, Brattling joined a patrol of eleven cavalrymen of Company C, 8th Cavalry Regiment, at Fort Belden, New Mexico, in pursuit of a band of hostile Indians who had attacked nearby settlers and stolen their cattle. The patrol caught up with the Indians on July 10 in a canyon near Fort McRae. In the ensuing battle Brattling was mortally wounded. He was posthumously awarded the Medal of Honor for "services against hostile Indians."

Initially buried in the Fort McRae, New Mexico, post cemetery, his remains and those of others were removed thirteen years later and buried in an "unknown" grave at Fort Leavenworth, Kansas. This fact was not discovered until 2001, when a document was found in the National Archives about the reinternment. Until that time it was believed that Brattling's remains were still at Fort McRae, which was now underwater after the construction of the Elephant Lake Reservoir that had begun in 1911. In 2003 the Congressional Medal of Honor Society erected a monument to Brattling on the east side of the lake near the old fort. A memorial to Brattling is in the Fort Bliss Cemetery in Section MA, Grave 29.

Cpl. Benito Martinez (1932–1952)

Benito Martinez, born and educated in Fort Hancock, Texas, earned his medal on September 6, 1952, near Satac-ri, Korea, with the 1st Battalion, 27th Infantry Regiment, 25th Infantry Division.

He was mortally wounded in the action and was initially buried in his hometown cemetery. His remains were moved in the 1980s to the Fort Bliss National Cemetery. Elementary schools in both Fort Hancock and El Paso are named in his memory.

His citation states:

> Cpl. Martinez, a machine gunner with Company A, distinguished himself by conspicuous gallantry and outstanding courage above and beyond the call of duty in action against the enemy. While manning a listening post forward of the main line of resistance, his position was attacked by a hostile force of reinforced company strength. In the bitter fighting which ensued, the enemy infiltrated the defense perimeter and, realizing that encirclement was imminent, Cpl. Martinez elected to remain at his post in an attempt to stem the onslaught. In a daring defense, he raked the attacking troops with crippling fire, inflicting numerous casualties. Although contacted by sound power phone several times, he insisted that no attempt be made to rescue him because of the danger involved. Soon thereafter, the hostile forces rushed the emplacement, forcing him to make a limited withdrawal with only an automatic rifle and pistol to defend himself. After a courageous 6-hour stand and shortly before dawn, he called in for the last time, stating that the enemy was converging on his position His magnificent stand enabled friendly elements to reorganize, attack, and regain the key terrain. Cpl. Martinez' incredible valor and supreme sacrifice reflect lasting glory upon himself and are in keeping with the honored traditions of the military service.

(Section B, Grave 366A)

S. Sgt. Ambrosio Guillen (1929–1953)

Ambrosio Guillen, a native of Colorado who grew up in El Paso, earned his medal on July 25, 1953—two days before the Korean War ceasefire—while fighting with the 2nd Battalion, 7th Marine Regiment. He was killed in the action, and his body was escorted back to the Fort Bliss National Cemetery by his brother, who was also serving in the Far East. His citation states:

> For conspicuous gallantry and intrepidity at the risk of his life above and beyond the call of duty while serving as a platoon Sergeant of Company F, Second Battalion, Seventh Marines, First Marine Division (Reinforced), in action against enemy aggressor forces in Korea on July 25, 1953. Participating in the defense of an outpost forward of the main line of resistance, Staff Sergeant GUILLEN maneuvered his platoon over unfamiliar terrain in the face of hostile fire and placed his men in fighting positions. With his unit pinned down when the outpost was attacked under cover of darkness by an estimated force of two enemy battalions supported by mortar and artillery fire, he deliberately exposed himself to the heavy barrage and attacks to direct his men in defending their positions and personally supervise the treatment and evacuation of the wounded. Inspired by his leadership, the platoon quickly rallied and engaged the enemy force in fierce hand-to-hand combat. Although critically wounded during the course of the battle, Staff Sergeant Guillen refused medical aid and continued to direct his men throughout the remainder of the engagement until the enemy was defeated and thrown into disorderly retreat. Succumbing to his wounds within a few hours, Staff Sergeant GUILLEN, by his outstanding courage and indomitable fighting spirit, was directly responsible for the success of his platoon in repelling a numerically superior enemy force.

(Section E, Grave 9171)

M. Sgt. Victor Hugo Espinoza (1928–1986)

An El Paso native, Victor Hugo Espinoza was with the 23rd Infantry Regiment of the 2nd Infantry Division at Chorwon, Korea, on August 1, 1952. In a battle to secure "Old Baldy," Espinoza singlehandedly neutralized a machine gun and crew and destroyed an enemy tunnel, mortar position, and two bunkers. For his actions

Espinoza was awarded the Distinguished Service Cross, the army's second-highest medal for valor.

In 2014 the US Congress directed the Department of Defense to review the service records and decoration citations of Jewish and Hispanic Americans who may have deserved but been denied the Medal of Honor due to "racial prejudice." As a result, Espinoza's DSC was upgraded to the Medal of Honor on May 18, 2014. The citation states:

> Corporal Victor H. Espinoza distinguished himself by acts of gallantry and intrepidity above and beyond the call of duty while serving as an Acting Rifleman in Company A, 23d Infantry Regiment, 2d Infantry Division during combat operations against an armed enemy in Chorwon, Korea, on August 1, 1952. On that day, Corporal Espinoza and his unit were responsible for securing and holding a vital enemy hill. As the friendly unit neared its objective, it was subjected to a devastating volume of enemy fire, slowing its progress. Corporal Espinoza, unhesitatingly and being fully aware of the hazards involved, left his place of comparative safety and made a deliberate one-man assault on the enemy with his rifle and grenades, destroying a machinegun and killing its crew. Corporal Espinoza continued across the fire-swept terrain to an exposed vantage point where he attacked an enemy mortar position and two bunkers with grenades and rifle fire, knocking out the enemy mortar position and destroying both bunkers and killing their occupants. Upon reaching the crest, and after running out of rifle ammunition, he called for more grenades. A comrade who was behind him threw some Chinese grenades to him. Immediately upon catching them, he pulled the pins and hurled them into the occupied trenches, killing and wounding more of the enemy with their own weapons. Continuing on through a tunnel, Corporal Espinoza made a daring charge, inflicting at least seven more casualties upon the enemy who were fast retreating into the tunnel. Corporal Espinoza was quickly in pursuit, but the hostile fire from the opening prevented him from overtaking the retreating enemy. As a result, Corporal Espinoza destroyed the tunnel

with TNT, called for more grenades from his company, and hurled them at the enemy troops until they were out of reach. Corporal Espinoza's incredible display of valor secured the vital strong point and took a heavy toll on the enemy, resulting in at least fourteen dead and eleven wounded.

(Section F, Grave 1115)

Houston National Cemetery

Houston, Texas

Located fifteen miles northwest of downtown, the Houston National Cemetery is the only government cemetery constructed in the United States during the Vietnam War. Officially dedicated on December 7, 1965, the cemetery—at 419.2 acres—is only slightly smaller than Arlington National Cemetery, to which it is often compared.

The largest and most prominent feature on the grounds is its semicircular Hemicycle, containing a chapel, carillon, and speaker's stand. The horseshoe-shaped Hemicycle is one of only three in the National Cemetery System (the others are at Arlington National Cemetery and the Manila American Cemetery in the Philippines). Two sweeping arcs extend horizontally from the bell tower to envelop a semicircular courtyard with a capacity of 3,000 seated spectators. Each of the arcs has both upper- and lower-level walkways. The chapel contains mosaic

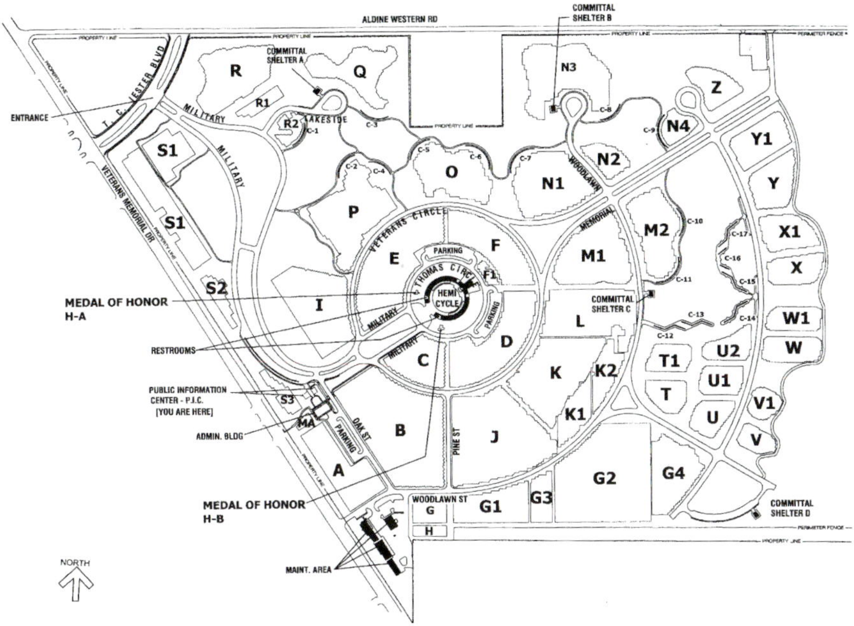
COMMITTAL SHELTER B
ALDINE WESTERN RD
COMMITTAL SHELTER A
ENTRANCE
T. C. JESTER BLVD
MILITARY
LAKESIDE
VETERANS MEMORIAL DR
VETERANS CIRCLE
PARKING
THOMAS CIRCLE
HEMI CYCLE
WOODLAWN
MEMORIAL
COMMITTAL SHELTER C
MEDAL OF HONOR H-A
RESTROOMS
PUBLIC INFORMATION CENTER - P.I.C. [YOU ARE HERE]
ADMIN. BLDG
OAK ST
PINE ST
WOODLAWN ST
MEDAL OF HONOR H-B
MAINT. AREA
COMMITTAL SHELTER D
NORTH
R
R1
R2
Q
N3
Z
N4
Y1
Y
X1
X
W1
W
V1
V
U2
U1
U
T1
T
S1
S2
S3
P
O
N1
N2
M1
M2
L
K
K1
K2
I
E
F
F1
D
C
B
A
MA
J
G
G1
G2
G3
G4
H

cut-glass windows that display the official seals of the VA and the branches of the armed forces. On May 30, 1970, a set of 305 hand-cast bells produced by the Schulmerich Company was added to the tower. Music from the bells can be heard throughout the cemetery and surrounding area. A portion of the grassy area of the Hemicycle and the circular driveway leading to it has been designated as the Medal of Honor section.

Notable Interments

Albert Richard Thomas (1898–1966)

Born in Nacogdoches, Texas, Albert Richard Thomas worked in his father's store before joining the army and serving as a lieutenant in World War I. When discharged, he attended and graduated from Rice Institute and the University of Texas Law School. He then practiced law in his hometown before moving to Houston to become an assistant US attorney. In 1936 he ran as a Democrat to become the congressman for the Eighth District of Texas, which included Houston and Harris County.

In that position he became a friend and protégé of fellow Texan Senator—and later President—Lyndon Johnson. As Thomas rose in rank and seniority in the Congress, he secured many defense and space programs for Houston, including the National Aeronautics and Space Administration's Manned Spacecraft Center (later named in honor of Johnson). Johnson would later say that the country has "a leadership in space which it wouldn't have without Albert Thomas."

Thomas accompanied Johnson and President Jack Kennedy to Texas in November 1963. He was aboard *Air Force One* when Johnson was sworn in as president after Kennedy's assassination.

Congressman Thomas was also instrumental in 1963 in securing the approval for the purchasing of the land that became the Houston National Cemetery. He died, after nearly thirty years in the US Congress, three months after the cemetery opened in 1966. He is buried in the mall area southwest of the Hemicycle. Johnson said of Thomas, "Of the qualities that made Albert Thomas a remarkable man, devotion to the people he served and loyalty to his friends stand higher than all. I knew him—and knew him well—for a long time. He loved Houston and the Congress of the United States. He worked hard. He served well. His death leaves a lonely place in the lives of those who knew him best."

Dan Robert Bankhead (1920–1976)

Dan (not Daniel, as listed in some sources) Robert Bankhead was the first African American pitcher in the major leagues. Born in Alabama, Bankhead played baseball in the Negro League before he joined the Marine Corps in World War II, where he rose in rank to sergeant. He returned to the Negro League diamonds after the war and in 1947 was signed by Branch Rickey and the Brooklyn Dodgers. On August 26 he made his initial major league appearance—the first by a black pitcher. In addition to pitching three and a third innings, Bankhead hit a homerun in his first time at bat. He also participated in the 1947 World Series.

Following the 1947 season, Bankhead went to the minor leagues before returning to Brooklyn in 1950 for two years. He finished his career playing in the Mexican League until his retirement in 1966. (Section B, Grave 2651)

Lt. Col. Kermit K. Beahan (1918–1989)

Born in Joplin, Missouri, Kermit K. Beahan attended Rice Institute on a football scholarship. He joined the Army Air Forces in 1939 to become a pilot but washed out of the training and became a bombardier instead. After flying thirty missions in B-17s over North Africa and Europe, he was transferred to instructor duty in Midland, Texas. There he was recruited by Col. Paul Tibbets to be a part of the 509th Composite Group, a unit of B-29s that was formed to deliver the atomic bombs over Japan.

On August 6, 1945, Beahan was aboard the *Great Artiste*, the blast instrumentation support plane on the first atomic mission that bombed Hiroshima. Three days later he was the bombardier aboard *Bockscar*, which dropped the second atomic bomb—this one on Nagasaki. After his retirement from the air force in 1964, Beahan worked as a technical writer for Brown and Root. In 1985 Beahan said that he would never apologize for dropping the bomb because it was the "best way out of a hell of a mess." He added that he hoped he would be the last bombardier to drop an atomic bomb on people. (Section K, Grave 389)

Goree C. Carter (1931–1990)

Born in Houston's Fifth Ward, Goree C. Carter taught himself how to play the guitar while working at the Comet Rice Mill. At age eighteen, Carter and his band, The Hepcats, signed with Sol Kahal's Freedom Records in Houston and recorded several songs. Their 1949 recording of "Rock Awhile," with Goree's overdriven electric guitar style, is credited by many as being "the first rock and roll record." His leading riff strongly resembles the style later adopted by Chuck Berry.

In 1950, Goree was drafted into the US Army and served as a combat infantryman in the Korean War. His music career never took off after his discharge. Many of the major recording labels turned him down, saying he was "ahead of his time." He died at the age of fifty-nine in the same Fifth Ward home where he had been born. (Section J, Grave 731)

Willard Jessie Brown (1915–1996)

Nicknamed "Home Run" by his teammates, Willard Jessie Brown was the Louisiana native who played in the Negro League for ten years before joining the army and serving for two years as a Tec 5 during World War II. He returned to baseball after the war in the Negro League and briefly played in the majors with the St. Louis Browns in 1947. On July 20 he took the field with Hank Thompson—the first time two African Americans appeared together in a major league baseball game. Brown achieved another first on August 13 when he hit the first home-run by a black player in the American League.

After leaving baseball, Brown settled in Houston. He was elected to the Baseball Hall of Fame in 2006. (Section G-2, Grave 3906)

Medal of Honor Recipients

Capt. James H. Fields (1920–1970)

James H. Fields, born in Caddo, Texas, and a graduate of Mirabeau Lamar High School in Houston, was drafted into the army in 1942. He received an officer's commission in 1944 and was assigned as a platoon leader in A Company, 10th Armored Infantry Battalion of the 4th Armored Division when he earned his Medal of Honor. After personally awarding the medal to Fields, Gen. George S. Patton Jr. sent him back to the United States. General Patton explained in his book, *War as I Knew It*, "I did not want Lieutenant Fields sent to the front anymore, because it has been my unfortunate observation that whenever a man gets the Medal of Honor or even the Distinguished Service Cross, he usually attempts to outdo himself and gets killed, whereas, in order to produce a virile race, such men should be kept alive."

After the war, Fields returned to Texas where he was an independent oil operator.

His citation states:

> For conspicuous gallantry and intrepidity at risk of life above and beyond the call of duty, at Rechicourt, France. On September 27, 1944, during a sharp action with the enemy infantry and tank forces, 1st Lt. Fields personally led his platoon in a counterattack on the enemy position. Although his platoon had been seriously depleted, the zeal and fervor of his leadership was such as to inspire his small force to accomplish their mission in the face of overwhelming enemy opposition. Seeing that 1 of the men had been wounded, he left his slit trench and with complete disregard for his personal safety attended the wounded man and administered first aid. While returning to his slit trench he was seriously wounded by a shell burst, the fragments of which cut through his face and head, tearing his teeth, gums, and nasal passage. Although rendered speechless by his wounds, 1st Lt. Fields refused to be evacuated and continued to lead his platoon by the use of hand signals. On 1 occasion, when 2 enemy machineguns had a portion of his unit under deadly crossfire, he left his hole, wounded as he was, ran to a light machinegun, whose crew had been knocked out, picked up the gun, and fired it from his hip with such deadly accuracy that both the enemy gun positions were silenced. His action so impressed his men that they found new courage to take up the fire fight, increasing their firepower, and exposing themselves more than ever to harass the enemy with additional bazooka and machinegun fire. Only when his objective had been taken and the enemy scattered did 1st Lt. Fields consent to be evacuated to the battalion command post. At this point he refused to move further back until he had explained to his battalion commander by drawing on paper the position of his men and the disposition of the enemy forces. The dauntless and gallant heroism displayed by 1st Lt. Fields were largely

responsible for the repulse of the enemy forces and contributed in a large measure to the successful capture of his battalion objective during this action. His eagerness and determination to close with the enemy and to destroy him was an inspiration to the entire command, and are in the highest traditions of the U.S. Armed Forces.

(Section H, Grave B6)

S. Sgt. Marcario Garcia (1920–1972)

Marcario Garcia (also known by Macario) was born in Villa de Castano in the state of Coahuila, Mexico, as one of nine children. At age three he accompanied his family to the United States, where they worked in the cotton fields around Sugar Land. He entered the army on November 11, 1942, and was wounded in the Normandy Invasion on D-Day in 1944. After recovering, he served as a squad leader in Company B, 1st Battalion, 22nd Infantry Regiment of the 4th Infantry Division, with which he earned his medal on November 27, 1944, near Grosshau, Germany.

After returning home from the war, Garcia was wearing his uniform when he was denied service in a café in Richmond, Texas, because he was Mexican. Garcia argued with the café owner, who called the police and had the Medal of Honor recipient arrested. He became an icon for Americans' discrimination against Hispanics, and several state and national organizations came to his support.

Garcia was granted US citizenship in 1947. He worked as a counselor in the Houston Veterans Administration until his death in an automobile accident in 1972. A section of Houston's 69th Street is named in his honor, as is the city's Army Reserve Center. A middle school in Sugar Land also bears his name.

His citation states:

> While an acting squad leader of Company B, 22d Infantry, on 27 November 1944, near Grosshau, Germany, he single-handedly assaulted two enemy machinegun emplacements. Attacking prepared positions on a wooded hill, which could be approached only through meager cover, his company was pinned down by intense machinegun fire and subjected to a concentrated artillery and mortar barrage. Although painfully wounded, he refused to be evacuated and on his own initiative crawled forward alone until he reached a position near an enemy emplacement. Hurling grenades, he boldly assaulted the position, destroyed the gun, and with his rifle killed three of the enemy who attempted to escape. When he rejoined his company, a second machinegun opened fire and again the intrepid soldier went forward, utterly disregarding his own safety. He stormed the position and destroyed the gun, killed three more Germans, and captured four prisoners. He fought on with his unit until the objective was taken and only then did he permit himself to be removed for medical care. S/Sgt. (then private) Garcia's conspicuous heroism, his inspiring, courageous conduct, and his complete disregard for his personal safety wiped out two enemy emplacements and enabled his company to advance and secure its objective.

(Section H, Grave A1)

1st Lt. Raymond L. Knight (1922–1945)

Raymond L. Knight joined the Army Air Forces after graduating from John Reagan High School (now Heights High School) in Houston. By 1945 he was a decorated veteran pilot flying against the Germans in northern Italy. A month before the war ended, as a part of the 346th Fighter Squadron of the 350th Fighter

Group, he led repeated attacks against German air bases that earned him the Medal of Honor. The medal was presented to his widow and two-year-old son on the stage of Reagan High School, upon which he had walked as a graduate only five years earlier. Knight's remains were moved from Italy to Houston's Woodlawn Garden of Memories in 1949 and then moved again to the Medal of Honor section of the Houston National Cemetery on April 25, 1992.

His citations states:

> Knight piloted a fighter-bomber aircraft in a series of low-level strafing missions, destroying 14 grounded enemy aircraft and leading attacks which wrecked 10 others during a critical period of the Allied drive in northern Italy. On the morning of 24 April, he volunteered to lead two other aircraft against the strongly defended enemy airdrome at Ghedi. Ordering his fellow pilots to remain aloft, he skimmed the ground through a deadly curtain of antiaircraft fire to reconnoiter the field, locating eight German aircraft hidden beneath heavy camouflage. He rejoined his flight, briefed them by radio, and then led them with consummate skill through the hail of enemy fire in a low-level attack, destroying five aircraft, while his flight accounted for two others. Returning to his base, he volunteered to lead three other aircraft in reconnaissance of Bergamo airfield, an enemy base near Ghedi and 1 known to be equally well defended. Again ordering his flight to remain out of range of antiaircraft fire, 1st Lt. Knight flew through an exceptionally

intense barrage, which heavily damaged his Thunderbolt, to observe the field at minimum altitude. He discovered a squadron of enemy aircraft under heavy camouflage and led his flight to the assault. Returning alone after this strafing, he made 10 deliberate passes against the field despite being hit by antiaircraft fire twice more, destroying six fully loaded enemy twin-engine aircraft and two fighters. His skillfully led attack enabled his flight to destroy four other twin-engine aircraft and a fighter plane. He then returned to his base in his seriously damaged plane. Early the next morning, when he again attacked Bergamo, he sighted an enemy plane on the runway. Again he led three other American pilots in a blistering low-level sweep through vicious antiaircraft fire that damaged his plane so severely that it was virtually nonflyable. Three of the few remaining enemy twin-engine aircraft at that base were destroyed. Realizing the critical need for aircraft in his unit, he declined to parachute to safety over friendly territory and unhesitatingly attempted to return his shattered plane to his home field. With great skill and strength, he flew homeward until caught by treacherous air conditions in the Apennine Mountains, where he crashed and was killed. The gallant action of 1st Lt. Knight eliminated the German aircraft which were poised to wreak havoc on Allied forces pressing to establish the first firm bridgehead across the Po River; his fearless daring and voluntary self-sacrifice averted possible heavy casualties among ground forces and the resultant slowing on the German drive culminated in the collapse of enemy resistance in Italy.

(Section H, Grave B11)

1st Sgt. David H. McNerney (1931–2010)

Born in Massachusetts to a father who was a highly decorated veteran of World War II, David H. McNerney moved to Houston as a child and graduated from St. Thomas High School. After graduation he enlisted in the navy and served two tours in the Korean War. He then enrolled in the University of Houston but soon dropped out and joined the army. McNerney rose in rank to first sergeant as he served a tour in Vietnam as an advisor and then two tours with Company A, 1st Battalion, 8th Infantry Regiment, 4th Infantry Division. He earned his Medal of Honor in the Battle of Polei Doc on March 22, 1967, when he took command of his company's survivors after all its officers were killed or wounded.

McNerney returned to Vietnam for a fourth tour before retiring in 1969. He settled in Crosby and worked at the Port of Houston as a customs inspector.

His citation states:

> 1st Sgt. McNerney distinguished himself when his unit was attacked by a North Vietnamese battalion near Polei Doc. Running through the hail of enemy fire to the area of heaviest contact, he was assisting in the development of a defensive perimeter when he encountered several enemy at close range. He killed the enemy but was painfully injured when blown from his feet by a grenade. In spite of this injury, he assaulted and destroyed an enemy machinegun position that had pinned down five of his comrades beyond the defensive line. Upon learning his commander and artillery forward observer had been killed, he assumed command of the company. He adjusted artillery fire to within 20 meters of the position in a daring measure to repulse enemy assaults. When the smoke grenades used to mark the position were gone, he moved into a nearby clearing to designate the location to friendly aircraft. In spite of enemy fire he remained exposed until he was certain the position was spotted and then climbed into a tree and tied the identification panel to its highest branches. Then he moved among

his men readjusting their position, encouraging the defenders and checking the wounded. As the hostile assaults slackened, he began clearing a helicopter landing site to evacuate the wounded. When explosives were needed to remove large trees, he crawled outside the relative safety of his perimeter to collect demolition material from abandoned rucksacks. Moving through a fusillade of fire he returned with the explosives that were vital to the clearing of the landing zone. Disregarding the pain of his injury and refusing medical evacuation, First Sgt. McNerney remained with his unit until the next day when the new commander arrived.

(Section H, Grave A4)

Dallas–Fort Worth National Cemetery

Dallas, Texas

The Dallas–Fort Worth National Cemetery, the newest national veterans burial ground in Texas, overlooks picturesque Mountain Creek Lake. Set among rolling green hills with the spires of Dallas Baptist University visible to its southwest, this site is one of the most beautiful cemeteries in Texas, if not *the* most beautiful. Dedicated in 2000, it contains 638.4 acres, of which 152 acres have been developed as of 2016. When fully developed, it will have burial space for more than 280,000 veterans.

Veterans Lake in the eastern part of the cemetery contributes to the peace and beauty of the Dallas–Fort Worth National Cemetery. A memorial walkway surrounds the lake and provides an area where various military and civic organizations can erect

DALLAS - FORT WORTH NATIONAL CEMETERY

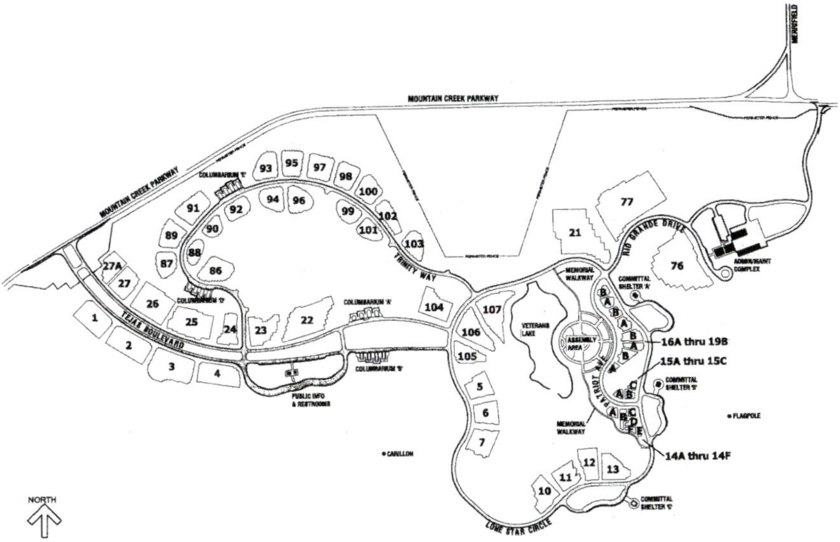

monuments focused on the events and participants in America's wars of the twentieth century. There are currently fifty such memorials in place.

Notable Interments

Capt. Cloyde C. Pinson Sr. (1922–2006) and Pfc. Cloyde C. Pinson Jr. (1946–1967)

Cloyde Pinson Sr., born in Ohio, entered the army in 1941 and served in North Africa and Italy during World War II. After the war he transferred to the air force and took part in the Berlin Airlift before retiring as a captain after twenty-one years of active duty. He then worked for twenty-two years at General Dynamics in Fort Worth. After his second retirement, Pinson Sr. focused on the creation of a national veterans cemetery in North Texas. By 1989 he had become the chairperson of the Texas National Cemetery Foundation and was instrumental in the approval for and establishment of the Dallas–Fort Worth National Cemetery.

Cloyde C. Pinson Jr. was born in New Orleans and killed by hostile fire while a member of D Company, 1st Battalion, 1st Marine Division, in Quang Nam Province, South Vietnam, on May 12, 1967. He was buried in the Laurel Land Cemetery in Dallas.

The Dallas–Fort Worth National Cemetery was officially dedicated thirty-three years to the day after Pinson Jr. was killed. His remains were disinterred from Laurel Land on April 12, 2006, and reburied in the cemetery his father had helped establish. Two days after the reburial, Pinson Sr. died. Today he rests next to his son. (Pinson Sr., Section 76, Grave 1702B; Pinson Jr., Section 76, Grave 1702A)

George Allen “Pat” Summerall (1930–2013)

George Allen “Pat” Summerall, born in Florida, was an army veteran of the Korean War era who played football at the University of Arkansas and then in the National Football League for ten seasons. He went on to a forty-year career as a sports commentator and announced sixteen Super Bowls, twenty-six Masters Tournaments, and twenty-one US Opens. His deep, distinctive voice made him one of the most recognized figures on TV and radio. (Columbarium D, Row CT1, Site D79)

Glenn Edward McDuffie (1927–2014)

Glenn Edward McDuffie left his home in North Carolina at age fifteen and lied about his age to join the navy during World War II. On August 14, 1945, he was in New York’s Time Square when the surrender of Japan was announced. In the jubilation on the street, McDuffie grabbed a willing female stranger in a white dress and kissed her. Photographer Alfred Eisenstaedt caught the kiss on his camera. That kiss appeared in *Life* magazine and other media to become the symbol of the spontaneous happiness brought about by the end of the war.

Over the years there have been several veterans who claimed to be the "kissing sailor." McDuffie is the only one whose claim is supported by forensic analysis, performed by Lois Gibson, a forensic artist with the Houston Police Department.

After his discharge, McDuffie played semipro baseball and worked for the US Postal Service. His headstone includes the inscription "VJ Day Kissing Sailor." (Section 17B, Grave 281)

Patricio "Patrick" E. Zamarripa (1983–2016)

After graduation from R. L. Paschal High School in Fort Worth, Patricio "Patrick" E. Zamarripa joined the army and over the next eight years served three tours of duty in Iraq. After his discharge he joined the Dallas Police Department. On July 7, 2016, Zamarripa was one of five Dallas police officers killed by a racist sniper—the deadliest attack on US law enforcement officers since the assaults of 9/11. (Section 76, Grave 1658S)

Medal of Honor Recipients

Col. James Lamar Stone (1922–2012)

James Lamar Stone graduated from the University of Arkansas in his native state in 1947 and moved to Houston to work at the General Electric Company. He was called to active duty as an infantry officer in 1948. On November 21, 1951, he was serving as a first lieutenant in Company E of the 2nd Battalion, 8th Cavalry Regiment, 1st Cavalry Division, on a hilltop outpost overlooking the Imjin River near Sokkogae, Korea. That night and the next morning, Stone earned his medal fighting against overwhelming numbers (48 against 800) of Chinese and then remaining behind to cover the withdrawal of his surviving platoon.

Stone was captured at the end of the battle and spent the next twenty-two months as a prisoner of war. After a cease-fire was declared and prisoners exchanged, Stone learned he was to receive the Medal of Honor. Choking back emotion, he said, "I don't deserve the medal. It should go to the men of my platoon."

After his release Stone remained on active duty and advanced in rank to colonel. He served a tour of duty in Vietnam. He retired to Arlington and later attended Veterans Day ceremonies at the Dallas–Fort Worth National Cemetery each year.

[*Author's Note*: The army is a large organization with hundreds of thousands of members—yet at the same time the paths of its soldiers seem to cross frequently. The author's brother, Jim Lanning, was an ROTC cadet training at summer camp at Fort Sill, Oklahoma, in the summer of 1963. Stone, then a major, was his tactical and evaluation officer. At camp's end, Jim celebrated a bit too much and missed bed check. This infraction might have cost him his regular army commission if Stone had not overlooked the incident and signed off on the RA recommendation. Jim went on to become a career officer. Details of the incident are covered in the author's *Texas Aggies in Vietnam: War Stories*.]

His citation states:

> 1st Lt. Stone, distinguished himself by conspicuous gallantry and indomitable courage above and beyond the call of duty in action against the enemy. When his platoon, holding a vital outpost position, was attacked by overwhelming Chinese forces, 1st Lt. Stone stood erect and exposed to the terrific enemy fire calmly directed his men in the defense. A defensive flame-thrower failing to function, he personally moved to its location, further exposing himself, and personally repaired

> the weapon. Throughout a second attack, 1st Lt. Stone; though painfully wounded, personally carried the only remaining light machine gun to place in the position in order to bring fire upon the Chinese advancing from two directions. Throughout he continued to encourage and direct his depleted platoon in its hopeless defense. Although again wounded, he continued the fight with his carbine, still exposing himself as an example to his men. When this final overwhelming assault swept over the platoon's position his voice could still be heard faintly urging his men to carry on, until he lost consciousness. Only because of this officer's driving spirit and heroic action was the platoon emboldened to make its brave but hopeless last ditch stand.

(Section 76, Grave 1658L)

Sgt. Candelario Garcia (1944–2013)

Candelario Garcia left his Corsicana, Texas, home on May 28, 1963, to enlist in the US Army. On December 8, 1968, he was an infantry team leader in the 1st Infantry Division when the unit became engaged in a pitched battle near Lai Khe, Vietnam. Garcia's actions in the fight earned him the Distinguished Service Cross. As a result of the Department of Defense review of valor decorations for Jewish and Hispanic Americans from World War II, the Korean War, and the Vietnam War, Garcia's award was upgraded to the Medal of Honor. It was posthumously awarded on March 14, 2014, and accepted by the command sergeant major of the 1st Infantry Division on behalf of surviving family members.

His citation states:

> Sergeant Candelario Garcia distinguished himself by acts of gallantry and intrepidity above and beyond the call of duty

while serving as an acting Team Leader for Company B, 1st Battalion, 2d Infantry, 1st Brigade,1st Infantry Division during combat operations against an armed enemy in Lai Khe, Republic of Vietnam, on December 8, 1968. On that day, while conducting reconnaissance, Sergeant Garcia and his platoon discovered communication wire and other signs of an enemy base camp leading into a densely vegetated area. As the men advanced, they came under intense fire. Several men were hit and trapped in the open. Ignoring a hail of hostile bullets, Sergeant Garcia crawled to within ten meters of a machinegun bunker, leaped to his feet and ran directly at the fortification, firing his rifle as he charged. Sergeant Garcia jammed two hand grenades into the gun port and then placed the muzzle of his weapon inside, killing all four occupants. Continuing to expose himself to intense enemy fire, Sergeant Garcia raced fifteen meters to another bunker and killed its three defenders with hand grenades and rifle fire. After again braving the enemies' barrage in order to rescue two casualties, he joined his company in an assault which overran the remaining enemy positions.

(Section 107, Grave 209)

THE STATE OF TEXAS

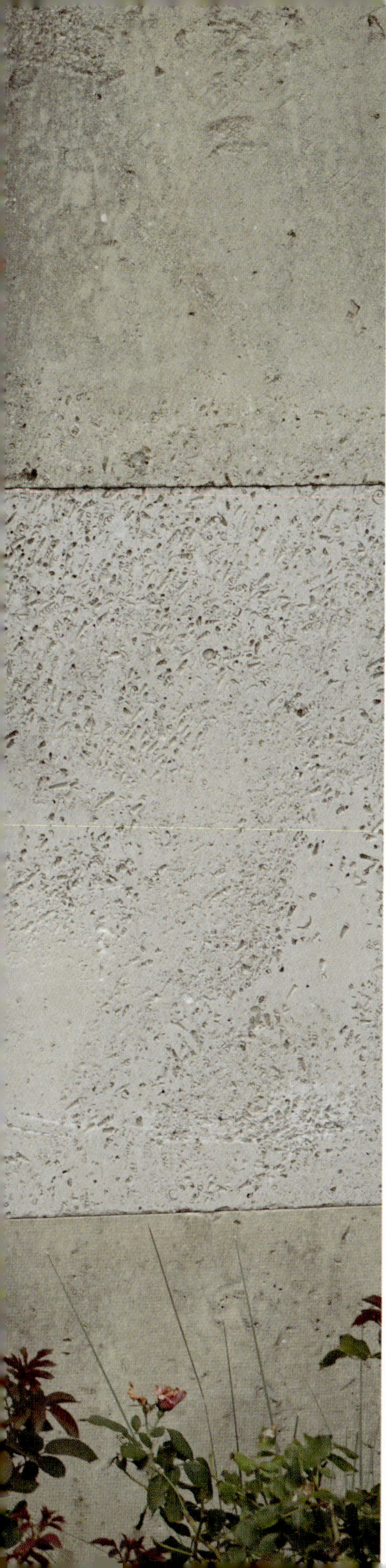

PART II

Texas State Veterans Cemeteries

AMONG CEMETERY administrators and workers as well as veterans themselves, free burial space and honors are known as "the last benefit" or "the last entitlement" for their service and sacrifice. Over the years the VA has sought to provide sufficient cemeteries across the United States so that there is one within seventy-five miles of every American veteran.

This seventy-five-mile guideline is fairly easy to meet in the smaller states as well as those with concentrated population centers. Although Texas has six national VA cemeteries, there are many resident veterans who live far from the current facilities. Those living near the borders of New Mexico, Oklahoma, Arkansas, and Louisiana may be within seventy-five-miles of a neighboring state's VA cemetery, but Texans, like veterans of all states, are loyal to their birthplaces and prefer to be buried in Texas soil.

With the mounting deaths of World War II and other veterans who did not reside near established VA cemeteries, the 75th Texas Legislature directed the Texas Veterans Commission in 1998 to commission a feasibility study for the funding and establishment for Texas state veterans cemeteries. The study confirmed that there was a need for such burial grounds and added that funding sources would have to be identified.

In 2000 the land commissioner and chairman of the Veterans Land Board, David Dewhurst, suggested that the state veterans loan programs be used as a funding source. A year later a statewide election approved Proposition 7 as "the Constitutional amendment authorizing the Veterans' Land Board to issue up to $500 million in general obligation bonds payable from the general revenues of the state for veterans' land and veterans' housing assistance funds to provide for veterans' cemeteries."

The 76th Texas Legislature then provided legislation under House Bill 310 to permit the Texas Veterans Land Board to build and operate up to a maximum of seven state veterans cemeteries. The bill also created a committee to determine the eligibility for criteria and to select cemetery sites. With the results, the Texas Veterans Land Board issued a request for proposals to cities for the donation of land across the state. Seven responses were received, and four were approved: Killeen, Abilene, Corpus Christi, and Mission. The first Texas veterans cemetery opened in 2006, with subsequent openings later in 2006 and in 2007 and 2010.

Each of the four communities provided the land for the cemeteries, while the costs of developing the facilities were shared by a partnership between the state and the US Department of Veterans Affairs. This amounted to a little more than $8 million per cemetery. Upon completion of construction, the Texas Veterans Land Board pays the operating costs. While the state Veterans Land Board continues to be in charge of the program, the day-to-day operation of the cemeteries is outsourced. Currently, Premier Cemetery Services of San Marcos is the contractor.

The Texas Veterans Land Board states that the cemeteries are "hallowed ground that are an expression of our respect for men and women who have served our nation with distinction. Texas State Veterans Cemeteries are special resting places, close to home, where friends, family and fellow Texans can honor Texas Veterans. The sacrifices they laid upon the alter of freedom can never be diminished or forgotten."

Central Texas State Veterans Cemetery

Killeen, Texas

The Central Texas State Veterans Cemetery, also known as the Texas State Cemetery at Killeen, is located southwest of the city and adjacent to the Fort Hood Military Reservation. Opened in January 2006, it is the first of the four cemeteries built and administered by the Texas Veterans Land Board. The site consists of 174 acres that were donated by Fort Hood. With about sixty interments per month, the cemetery is the most active of the Texas facilities.

Of the more than 6,000 interments since its opening until May 2015, 65 percent have been burials and 35 percent cremations with remains placed in the cemetery's columbarium. It is anticipated that the number of burials will total more than 27,000 within twenty years. Plans for expansion are already ongoing.

CLARENCE
TAYLOR
THURMAN
BEAVERS SR

CURTIS
FLOYD
OLIVER
JOE
JOYNER JR
ECOLIA A
DUNN
NORMAN
RICE
RUFUS
CLARK
JAMES R
SILVERIO P
RAMIREZ
SHIRLEY
CONWAY
PAUL
WAYNE
HENRY

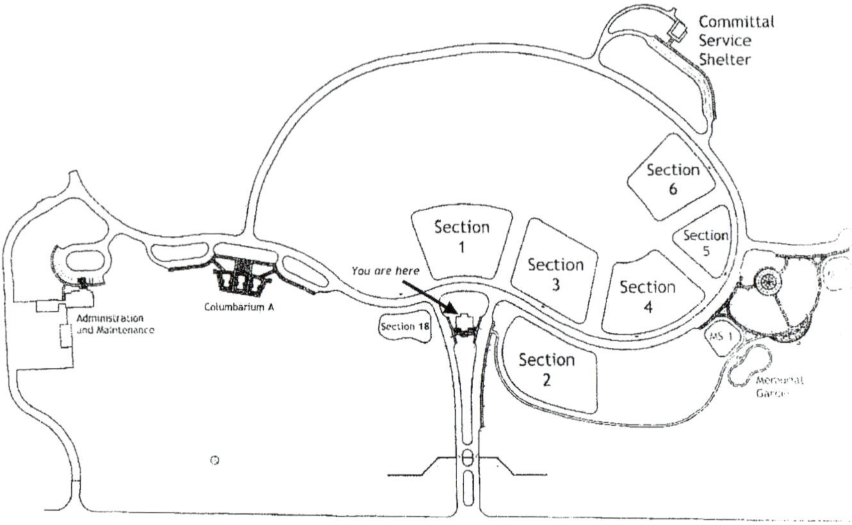
Committal
Service
Shelter
Section
6
Section
1
Section
5
Section
3
Section
4
You are here
Administration
and Maintenance
Columbarium A
Section 18
Section
2
MS 1

Central Texas Fallen Heroes Memorial Committee Founding Members
Patrick Turck - President
Jack St John - Vice President
Special Thanks
Killeen Monument Company - Jack Welch/CHAMPS - City of Killeen
Jack Chapman/Cosper Construction - Central Texas Community

Notable Interments

Maj. Gen. Stewart C. Meyer (1921–2013)

Stewart C. Meyer, born in El Paso, graduated from the US Military Academy at West Point and served in World War II, in which he fought as an artilleryman across Europe. He often said that his most traumatic experience of the war was the liberation of prisoners in a Nazi death camp. Meyer also served in the Korean and Vietnam Wars, earning a Silver Star, Purple Heart, and five Bronze Stars. Near the end of his career, he commanded the Operational Test Command at West Fort Hood. After his retirement he settled in nearby Harker Heights, where he was elected city mayor in 1993 and served until 1997. (Section 2, Grave W-291)

Sgt. William Travis Barker (1929–1951)

William Travis Barker entered the service in Rockwall County, Texas, and served as a medic with the 503rd Field Artillery Battalion (a segregated unit of African Americans with white officers), 2nd Infantry Division. On December 1, 1950, Barker's unit was

overrun during Battle of the Ch'ongch'on River and was taken to the Puktong prisoner of war camp in North Korea. When prisoners were exchanged in 1953, Barker was not among the returning Americans. His fellow prisoners reported that Barker had died on February 18, 1951.

Following the war the remains of more than 800 unidentified American POWs were repatriated and buried in the Military Cemetery of the Pacific at the Punchbowl in Honolulu, Hawaii. Advanced DNA procedures identified Barker's remains in June 2011, and he was reburied in the Central Texas Veterans Cemetery on August 15, 2012. (Section 3, Grave N-337)

Sgt. 1st Cl. Billy David Hill (1946–1968)

Born in Kansas, Billy David Hill lived in several places, including Texas and Nevada, before enlisting in the army. On January 21, 1968, he was acting as a door gunner on a UH-1D Huey with the 282nd Aviation Company, 14th Aviation Group, 1st Aviation Brigade, when his helicopter was shot down near Khe Sahn, South Vietnam. Survivors of the crash reported that Hill had likely been killed, but recovery efforts did not find his body. He was listed as Missing in Action until a review board declared him dead, body not recovered, on December 15, 1975. While in MIA status, he was promoted from staff sergeant to sergeant first class.

From 1993 to 2014, seven investigations were conducted on the whereabouts of Hill's remains. In 2015 the Department of Defense announced that it had "reanalyzed unknown remains returned from Vietnam during a unilateral turnover in 1989, which were reportedly recovered in the vicinity of Khe Sahn." DNA testing positively identified the remains as those of Hill.

Hill was buried in the Central Texas Veterans Cemetery on December 17, 2015—forty-eight years after his death. An article in the *Killeen Daily Herald* quoted Hill's cousin Beverly Jacobs, who lived in Gatesville, Texas, with his ninety-one-year-old father, as saying, "I think our mourning and grieving we took care of many years ago. This is more like a celebration of his life. He's a Texas boy. He wanted to come home to Texas and that's being accomplished. The great thing is he had 21 years of action, enjoying every minute of it. He was a gung-ho soldier. He loved his troops. He loved the army. He was patriotic. He loved his family and he was always laughing. He had a good life." (Section 4, Grave A-17)

Rio Grande Valley State Veterans Cemetery

Mission, Texas

Bentsen Palm Limited, a part of Rhodes Enterprises of Mission, donated seventy-five acres of a former cotton field near the Rio Grande for one of the four new state cemeteries. Thirty-one acres had been developed by December 2006, including administration and maintenance buildings as well as a committal service shelter, columbarium, and welcome center. The architecture of the structures incorporates the stucco and red tile style common to the Rio Grande Valley. At its formal opening, Secretary of Veterans Affairs Jim Nicholson said, "It is an honor for the Department of Veterans Affairs to partner with the people of Texas to build this shrine for our veterans. This new state cemetery will stand as a tribute to the men and women of Texas who have honorably served our nation."

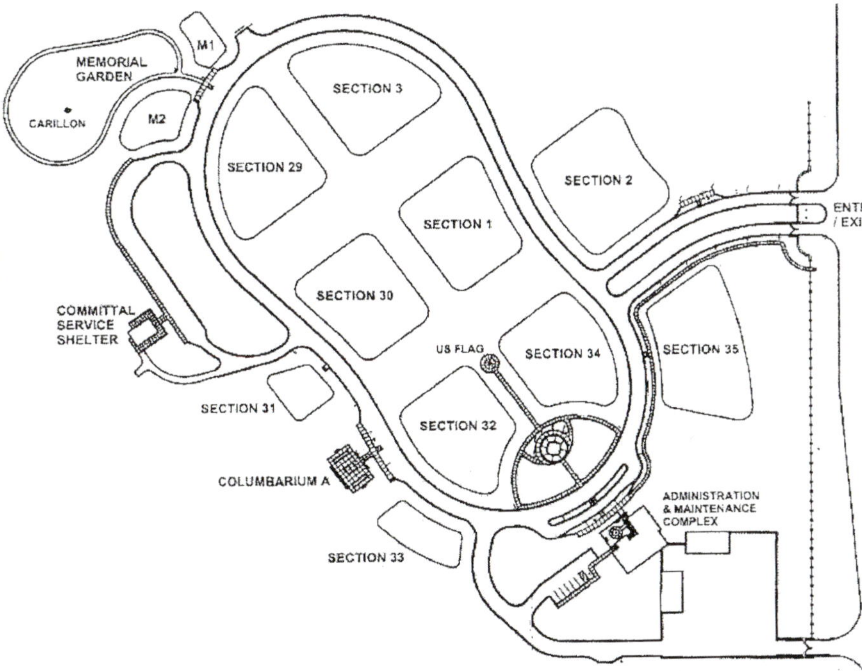
MEMORIAL
GARDEN
CARILLON
M1
M2
SECTION 3
SECTION 29
SECTION 2
ENTRY
/ EXIT
SECTION 1
SECTION 30
COMMITTAL
SERVICE
SHELTER
US FLAG
SECTION 34
SECTION 35
SECTION 31
SECTION 32
COLUMBARIUM A
ADMINISTRATION
& MAINTENANCE
COMPLEX
SECTION 33

ROBERTO C DELGADO
CANDELARIO GUTIERREZ
US ARMY
ALWAYS IN OUR HEARTS LOVE YOU
LEO G MARTINEZ JR
SGT
USAAF
WORLD WAR II
IN LOVING MEMORY
DAVID FOLIN
ADALBERTO PONCE
JUAN RODRIGUEZ

GONZALEZ
JOSEPH H JR
PFC USA
VIETNAM
1955 2010
HE LOVED GOD AND COUNTRY
THOMPSON
DARREL WAYNE
VIETNAM
1941 2010
SEMPER FI
WELLS
CHINGO
FRANCIS D
WORLD WAR II
AIRMANS MEDAL
ABIDE WITH ME
STOY
GEORGE THOMAS
TOGETHER FOREVER
GASKINS
GREENE
HOCHBAUM
JOHNSON
MACIAS
ZUNIGA
TOGETHER FOREVER

When fully developed, the cemetery will have the capacity for 25,000 interments. There is also additional adjacent land for expansion if necessary. The cemetery serves an estimated population of 45,000 veterans who live within seventy-five miles of the facility, a service area that is not exact because the cemetery accepts the remains of any qualified veteran. Included are vets who "wintered" in the Valley from their northern homes as well as Americans who live across the border in Mexico.

Notable Interments

Refugio C. Tamayo (1931–1950)

Refugio C. Tamayo grew up in San Benito, Texas, before entering the army during the Korean War. On December 12, 1950, he was a member of Company I of the 31st Regimental Combat Team, 7th Infantry Division, during the Battle of the Chosin Reservoir. His unit was overrun by a vastly larger number of Chinese soldiers. Many of the remains of the American dead, including Tamayo, were not recovered, and he was listed as Missing in Action.

On September 9, 2014, a memorial marker was placed in the Rio Grande Valley Texas Veterans State Cemetery in his honor. (Southern Memorial Section, Site D-30)

Texas State Veterans Cemetery at Abilene

Abilene, Texas

The Texas State Cemetery at Abilene became the third state veterans cemetery when it held its opening ceremonies on Memorial Day, May 25, 2009. Jerry Patterson, a US Marine veteran and the chairperson of the Texas Veterans Land Board, said to the 1,500 people who attended the dedication, "Today is not about a sale at the mall or a day off from work. Today is about honoring the soldiers who served our country with dignity and courage—and I'm proud to stand among so many fellow Texans who share my commitment to never forget their sacrifice."

Located on the southern shore of Lake Fort Phantom near Abilene, the sixty-three-acre facility will have a capacity of more than 40,000 burials when fully developed. It features an administration and visitor center; a covered, open-air structure for committal services; an assembly area for special occasions; and a memorial walkway for monuments to units and groups. Design

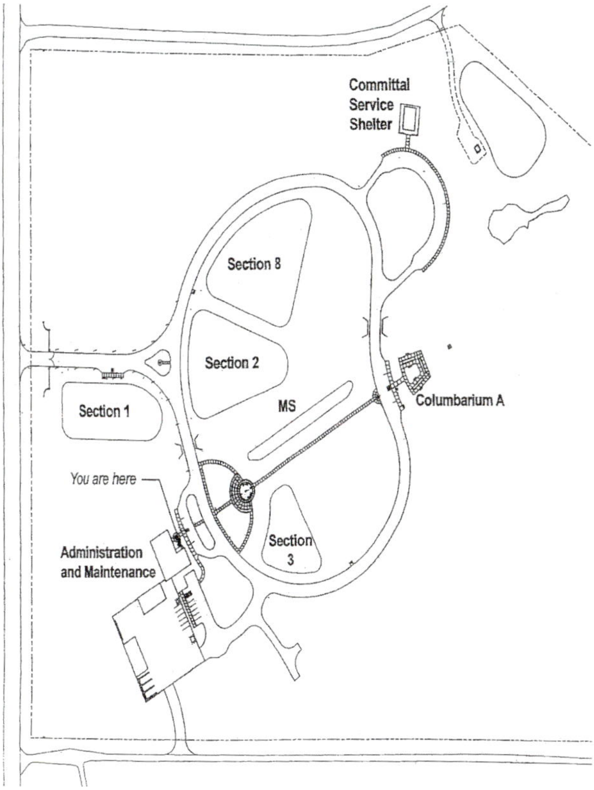
Committal
Service
Shelter
Section 8
Section 2
Section 1
MS
Columbarium A
You are here
Section 3
Administration
and Maintenance

of the cemetery reflects its West Texas location with a straightforward use of brick and native plant materials. Its xeriscaped grounds follow the region's climate challenges, incorporating the need for a respectful setting while still conserving maintenance and water resources.

Of particular note is the cemetery's main flagpole. On April 30, 2015, the Military Partnership of West Central Texas and the 12th Armored Division Memorial Museum rededicated the flagpole that had originally stood at nearby Camp Barkeley during World War II. Camp Barkeley, established southwest of Abilene in July of 1941, trained more than 60,000 troops, including the 45th and 19th Infantry Divisions and the 11th and 12th Armored Divisions, before its closure in September of 1945. Famed cartoonist Bill Mauldin began his career on the staff of the camp's newspaper.

Notable Interments

Lt. Col. Charles Weldon Kirk (1925–2009)

Charles Weldon Kirk, a native of Gorman, Texas, flew with the US Army Air Corps during World War II and continued to serve in the US Air Force Reserves for a total of twenty-three years. He began his law career in 1950 in Sweetwater and for nearly a half century served as an attorney and judge in the city and at the Nolan County Courthouse. From 1958 to 1998, he was the presiding judge of the 7th Administrative Judicial Region and from 1971 to 2000 the senior judge of the 32nd District Court. (Section 2A, Grave 11)

Coastal Bend State Veterans Cemetery

Corpus Christi, Texas

Opening on December 7, 2011, the Coastal Bend Veterans Cemetery is the newest of the Texas state veterans cemeteries. Located just off Interstate 37 northwest of downtown Corpus Christi, the cemetery has a master plan that calls for providing 31,500 gravesites over the next forty years.

Its fifty-four acres were donated by Flint Hills Resources, a chemical and biofuel company. Unlike most other national veterans cemeteries, Coastal Bend does not inter its veterans in neat angled rows. Rather, the cemetery is laid in repeating circles.

The Coastal Bend State Veterans Cemetery is the first veterans facility in the country to have an Unaccompanied Veteran Community Notification Program. When an indigent, homeless, or without-family veteran dies, the cemetery dispatches a mass

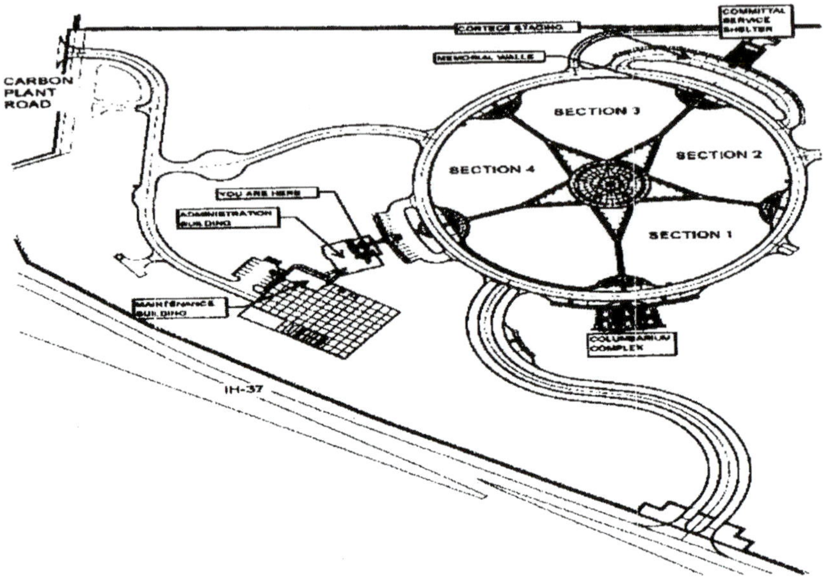
CARBON PLANT ROAD
CORTEGE STAGING
COMMITTAL SERVICE SHELTER
MEMORIAL WALLS
SECTION 3
SECTION 4
SECTION 2
SECTION 1
YOU ARE HERE
ADMINISTRATION BUILDING
MAINTENANCE BUILDING
COLUMBARIUM COMPLEX
IH-37

e-mail invitation to the general public, local media, and area veterans organizations as well as to city, county, and state leaders. As many as 400 people have attended one of the funerals.

Notable Interments

Pvt. Reynaldo G. Chacon (1935–2009)

Reynaldo Chacon, an army veteran from Corpus Christi, was the cemetery's first interment when he was buried on December 13, 2011. (Section 2, Grave A-1)

Cpl. Lucio R. Aguilar (1930–1953)

Lucio R. Aguilar, a native of Brownville, was an infantryman in the 35th Infantry Regiment of the 25th Infantry Division defending positions at Yongsan-dong, North Korea, about ten miles north of the Ch'ongch'on River on November 27, 1950. A massive attack by Chinese infantry forced Aguilar's unit to withdraw under heavy fire. The next day Aguilar was reported Missing in Action.

No further information about Aguilar was forthcoming, and after the truce and cease-fire a military review board on December 31, 1953, changed his status from missing to presumed dead. In 1956 the army declared that his remains were unrecoverable. Between 1991 and 1994, North Korea turned over 208 boxes of what were believed to contain the remains of an estimated 350–400 missing Americans. The Joint POW/MIA Accounting Command and Armed Forces DNA Laboratory used the location of where one set of remains was recovered, along with mitochondrial DNA from his sister and nephew, to match Aguilar.

On June 13, 2014, Aguilar was finally laid to rest with full military honors among his fellow veterans—more than a half century after he fell in battle fighting for his state and country. (Section 3F, Grave 249)

Sgt. Leopoldo L. Ruiz (1929–1950)

Leopoldo L. Ruiz, from Corpus Christi, was serving with Company K, 3rd Battalion, 31st Infantry Regiment of the 7th Infantry Division, near the Chosin Reservoir in North Korea in early December 1950 when his unit was overrun by a large Chinese force. Ruiz was declared missing on December 2 and presumed dead on December 12. His remains have never been recovered. On December 15, 2014, a memorial marker was placed in the Costal Bend cemetery in his honor.

The battle near Chosin Reservoir in December 1950 in which Ruiz was killed was the same fight in which Refugio Tamayo, who has a memorial marker in the Rio Grande Valley State Veterans Cemetery, was declared missing in action. (Section MW-1, Site A-1)

Appendix A

Eligibility Requirements for Burial in a National Cemetery

The National Cemetery Scheduling Office has the primary responsibility for verifying eligibility for burial in VA national cemeteries. A determination of eligibility is made in response to a request for burial in a VA national cemetery. To schedule a burial, fax all discharge documentation to 1-866-900-6417 and follow up with a phone call to 1-800-535-1117.

Persons Eligible for Burial in a National Cemetery

Veterans and Members of the Armed Forces (Army, Navy, Air Force, Marine Corps, Coast Guard)

(1) Any member of the armed forces of the United States who dies on active duty.

(2) Any veteran who was discharged under conditions other than dishonorable. With certain exceptions, service beginning after September 7, 1980, as an enlisted person and service after October 16, 1981, as an officer must be for a minimum of 24 continuous months or the full period for which the person was called to active duty (as in the case of a reservist called to active duty for a limited duration). Undesirable, bad conduct and any other type of discharge

other than honorable may or may not qualify the individual for veterans benefits, depending upon a determination made by a VA Regional Office. Cases presenting multiple discharges of varying character are also referred for adjudication to a VA Regional Office.

(3) Any citizen of the United States who, during any war in which the United States has or may be engaged, served in the armed forces of any government allied with the United States during that war, whose last active service was terminated honorably by death or otherwise and who was a citizen of the United States at the time of entry into such service and at the time of death.

Members of Reserve Components and Reserve Officers' Training Corps

(1) Reservists and National Guard members who, at time of death, were entitled to retired pay under Chapter 1223, Title 10, United States Code, or would have been entitled, but for being under the age of 60. Specific categories of individuals eligible for retired pay are delineated in Section 12731 of Chapter 1223, Title 10, United States Code.

(2) Members of reserve components and members of the Army National Guard or the Air National Guard who die while hospitalized or undergoing treatment at the expense of the United States for injury or disease contracted or incurred under honorable conditions while performing active duty for training or inactive duty training or undergoing such hospitalization or treatment.

(3) Members of the Reserve Officers' Training Corps of the Army, Navy, or Air Force who die under honorable conditions while attending an authorized training

camp or on an authorized cruise, while performing authorized travel to or from that camp or cruise, or while hospitalized or undergoing treatment at the expense of the United States for injury or disease contracted or incurred under honorable conditions while engaged in one of those activities.

(4) Members of reserve components who, during a period of active duty for training, were disabled or died from a disease or injury incurred or aggravated in the line of duty or, during a period of inactive duty training, were disabled or died from an injury or certain cardiovascular disorders incurred or aggravated in the line of duty.

Commissioned Officers, National Oceanic and Atmospheric Administration

(1) A commissioned officer of the National Oceanic and Atmospheric Administration (formerly titled the Coast and Geodetic Survey and the Environmental Science Services Administration) with full-time duty on or after July 29, 1945.

(2) A commissioned officer who served before July 29, 1945, and
   (a) Was assigned to an area of immediate military hazard as determined by the Secretary of Defense while in time of war, or in a presidentially declared national emergency; or
   (b) Served in the Philippine Islands on December 7, 1941, and continuously in such islands thereafter.

Public Health Service

(1) A commissioned officer of the Regular or Reserve Corps of the Public Health Service who served on full-time duty on or after July 29, 1945. If the service of the particular Public Health Service officer falls within

the meaning of active duty for training, as defined in Section 101(22), Title 38, United States Code, he or she must have been disabled or died from a disease or injury incurred or aggravated in the line of duty.

(2) A commissioned officer of the Regular or Reserve Corps of the Public Health Service who performed full-time duty prior to July 29, 1945:
   (a) In time of war;
   (b) On detail for duty with the Army, Navy, Air Force, Marine Corps, or Coast Guard; or
   (c) While the service was part of the military forces of the United States pursuant to an Executive Order of the president.

(3) A commissioned officer serving on inactive-duty training as defined in Section 101(23), Title 38, United States Code, whose death resulted from an injury incurred or aggravated in the line of duty.

World War II Merchant Mariners

(1) US merchant mariners with oceangoing service during the period of armed conflict, December 7, 1941, to December 31, 1946. Prior to the enactment of Public Law 105-368, US merchant mariners with oceangoing service during the period of armed conflict of December 7, 1941, to August 15, 1945, were eligible. With enactment of Public Law 105-368, the service period is extended to December 31, 1946, for those dying on or after November 11, 1998. A DD-214 documenting this service may be obtained by submitting an application to Commandant (G-MVP-6), US Coast Guard, 2100 2nd Street, SW, Washington, DC 20593. Notwithstanding, the mariner's death must have occurred on or after the enactment of Public Law 105-368.

(2) US merchant mariners who served on blockships in support of Operation Mulberry during World War II.

The Philippine Armed Forces

(1) Any Philippine veteran who was a citizen of the United States or an alien lawfully admitted for permanent residence in the United States at the time of his or her death and who resided in the United States at the time of his or her death; and

  (a) Was a person who served before July 1, 1946, in the organized military forces of the government of the Commonwealth of the Philippines while such forces were in the service of the armed forces of the United States pursuant to the military order of the president dated July 26, 1941, including organized guerilla forces under commanders appointed, designated, or subsequently recognized by the commander in chief, Southwest Pacific Area, or other competent authority in the US Army and who died on or after November 1, 2000; or

  (b) Was a person who enlisted between October 6, 1945, and June 30, 1947, with the armed forces of the United States with the consent of the Philippine government, pursuant to Section 14 of the Armed Forces Voluntary Recruitment Act of 1945, and who died on or after December 16, 2003.

Spouses and Dependents

(1) The spouse, surviving spouse, or dependent of an eligible veteran or member of the armed forces may be eligible for interment in a national cemetery even if that veteran is not buried or memorialized in a national cemetery.

(2) The surviving spouse of an eligible veteran who had a subsequent remarriage to a nonveteran and whose death occurred on or after January 1, 2000, is eligible for burial in a national cemetery, based on his or her marriage to the eligible veteran.

(3) The minor children of an eligible veteran. For purpose of burial in a national cemetery, a minor child is a child who is unmarried and
   (a) Who is under 21 years of age; or
   (b) Who is under 23 years of age and pursuing a full-time course of instruction at an approved educational institution.

(4) The unmarried adult child of an eligible veteran. For purpose of burial in a national cemetery, an unmarried adult child is of any age but became permanently physically or mentally disabled and incapable of self-support before reaching 21 years of age or before reaching 23 years of age if pursuing a full-time course of instruction at an approved educational institution. Proper supporting documentation must be provided.

Parents

(1) Biological or adoptive parents who died after October 13, 2010, and whose biological or adoptive child was a service member:
   (a) Whose death occurred on or after October 7, 2001; and
   (b Whose death was the result of a hostile casualty or a training-related injury; and
   (c) Who is interred in a national cemetery in a gravesite with available space for subsequent interment; and
   (d) Who, at the time of the parent's death, had no spouse, surviving spouse, or child who is buried or who, upon death, may be eligible for burial in a national cemetery.

(2) The term "hostile casualty" means a person who, as a member of the armed forces, dies as the direct result of hostile action with the enemy while in combat,

while going to or returning from a combat mission if the cause of death was directly related to hostile action, or while hospitalized or undergoing treatment at the expense of the United States for injury incurred during combat, including a person killed mistakenly or accidentally by friendly fire directed at a hostile force or what is thought to be a hostile force. The term "hostile casualty" does not include a person who dies due to the elements, a self-inflicted wound, combat fatigue, or a friendly force while the person was absent without leave, was a deserter, had dropped-from-rolls status, or was voluntarily absent from a place of duty.

(3) The term "training-related injury" means an injury incurred by a member of the armed forces while performing authorized training activities in preparation for a combat mission.

Others

Such other persons or classes of persons as designated by the Secretary of Veterans Affairs (38 U.S.C. § 2402(6)) or the Secretary of Defense (Public Law 95-202§ 401; 38 CFR § 3.7(x)).

Persons Not Eligible for Burial in a National Cemetery

Former Spouses

A former spouse of an eligible individual whose marriage to that individual has been terminated by annulment or divorce, if not otherwise eligible.

Other Family Members

Family members of an eligible person except those defined as eligible in the section entitled "Spouses and Dependents."

Disqualifying Characters of Discharge

A person whose only separation from the armed forces was under dishonorable conditions or whose character of service results in a bar to veterans benefits.

Discharge from Draft

A person who was ordered to report to an induction station, but was not actually inducted into military service.

Persons Found Guilty of a Capital Crime

Under 38 U.S.C. § 2411, interment or memorialization in a VA national cemetery or in Arlington National Cemetery is prohibited if a person is convicted of a federal or state capital crime for which a sentence of imprisonment for life or the death penalty may be imposed and the conviction is final. Federal officials may not inter in veterans cemeteries persons who are shown by clear and convincing evidence to have committed a federal or state capital crime but were unavailable for trial due to death or flight to avoid prosecution. Federally funded state veterans cemeteries must also adhere to this law. This prohibition is also extended to furnishing a Presidential Memorial Certificate, a burial flag, and a headstone or marker.

Persons Convicted of Certain Sex Offenses

Under 38 U.S.C. § 2411, interment or memorialization in a VA national cemetery or in Arlington National Cemetery is prohibited if a person is convicted of a Tier III sex offense, who was sentenced to a minimum of life imprisonment, and whose conviction is final. Federally funded state and tribal-organization veterans cemeteries must also adhere to this law. This prohibition also applies to a Presidential Memorial Certificate, burial flag, and headstone and marker benefits.

Subversive Activities

Any person convicted of subversive activities after September 1, 1959, shall have no right to burial in a national cemetery from and after the date of commission of such offense, based on periods of active military service commencing before the date of the commission of such offense, nor shall another person be entitled to burial on account of such an individual. Eligibility will be reinstated if the president of the United States grants a pardon.

Active or Inactive Duty for Training

A person whose only service is active duty for training or inactive-duty training in the National Guard or a reserve component, unless the individual meets the eligibility criteria listed above in the section entitled "Members of Reserve Components and Reserve Officers' Training Corps."

Other Groups

Members of groups whose service has been determined by the Secretary of the Air Force under the provisions of Public Law 95-202 as not warranting entitlement to benefits administered by the Secretary of Veterans Affairs.

Appendix B

Eligibility Requirements for Burial in a Texas State Veterans Cemetery

Veterans and members of the armed forces

Certain members of reserve components and Reserve Officers' Training Corps

Commissioned officers of the National Oceanic and Atmospheric Administration and Public Health Services

World War II merchant marines

Philippine armed forces

Spouses and dependents (however, burial of dependent children is limited to unmarried children under 21 years old or 23 years old if a full-time student at an approved educational institution)

Eligibility requirements for a Texas state veterans cemetery are the same as for US Department of Veterans Affairs national cemeteries. Exact eligibility requirements can be seen at the Veterans Affairs website or by calling the VA's toll-free burial benefits number at 1-800-827-1000. If you have any questions about eligibility, please call the Texas Veterans Land Board toll-free at 1-800-252-VETS (8387).

Charges for Interment

Burial at a Texas state veterans cemetery is a benefit earned by veterans, their spouses, and eligible dependents for their dedicated service to our country. There is no charge for the interment of veterans, their spouses, and eligible dependents. The burial benefit includes military honors for veterans, the grave plot, the opening and closing of the grave, a concrete grave liner for casketed burials, a headstone or marker, presentation of the burial flag to the next of kin, a presidential certificate, playing of Taps, a gun salute, and perpetual care of the grave. The funeral home will obtain a burial flag to accompany the veteran's casket or urn and will assist with requesting military honors.

The burial benefit for veterans, their spouses, and eligible dependents does not cover funeral home charges such as the cost of a casket, cremation, viewing, flower cars, or transportation of the remains and family. However, if the veteran dies of a service-connected cause of death, the family may be eligible for reimbursement from the VA for some of the funeral home costs up to $2,000.

Military Service Documents

Military Service Records

Visit the National Archives to request your military service records online, by mail, or by fax. Records include DD214/Separation Documents, Personnel Records, and Medical Records.

Military Record Request—Standard Form 180 (SF-180)

Request your military record using the National Archives Standard Form 180 (SF-180).

Appendix C

The Bivouac of the Dead

Theodore O'Hara (1820–1867)

The muffled drum's sad roll has beat
  The soldier's last tattoo;
No more on Life's parade shall meet
  That brave and fallen few.
On Fame's eternal camping-ground
  Their silent tents are spread,
And Glory guards with solemn round
  The bivouac of the dead.

No rumor of the foe's advance
  Now swells upon the wind;
No troubled thought at midnight haunts
  Of loved ones left behind;
No vision of the morrow's strife
  The warrior's dream alarms;
No braying horn nor screaming fife
  At dawn shall call to arms.

Their shivered swords are red with rust;
  Their plumèd heads are bowed;
Their haughty banner, trailed in dust,
  Is now their martial shroud.
And plenteous funeral tears have washed

The red stains from each brow,
And the proud forms, by battle gashed,
Are free from anguish now.

The Neighing troop, the flashing blade,
The bugle's stirring blast,
The charge, the dreadful cannonade,
The din and shout are past;
Nor war's wild note, nor glory's peal,
Shall thrill with fierce delight
Those breasts that nevermore may feel
The rapture of the fight.

Like the fierce northern hurricane
That sweeps this great plateau,
Flushed with the triumph yet to gain,
Came down the serried foe,
Who heard the thunder of the fray
Break o'er the field beneath,
Knew well the watchword of that day
Was "Victory or Death."

Long had the doubtful conflict raged
O'er all that stricken plain,
For never fiercer fight had waged
The vengeful blood of Spain;
And still the storm of battle blew,
Still swelled the glory tide;
Not long our stout old chieftain knew,
Such odds his strength could bide.

'Twas in that hour his stern command
Called to a martyr's grave
The flower of his own belovèd land,
The nation's flag to save.
By rivers of their fathers' gore

His first-born laurels grew,
And well he deemed the sons would pour
Their lives for glory too.

Full many a norther's breath has swept
O'er Angostura's plain,
And long the pitying sky has wept
Above its mouldered slain.
The raven's scream or eagle's flight
Or shepherd's pensive lay,
Alone awakes each sullen height
That frowned o'er that dread fray.

Sons of the dark and bloody ground,
Ye must not slumber there,
Where stranger steps and tongues resound
Along the heedless air.
Your own proud land's heroic soil
Shall be your fitter grave;
She claims from war his richest spoil—
The ashes of her brave.

Thus 'neath their parent turf they rest,
Far from the gory field,
Borne to a Spartan mother's breast
On many a bloody shield;
The sunshine of their native sky
Smiles sadly on them here,
And kindred eyes and hearts watch by
The heroes' sepulchre.

Rest on, embalmed and sainted dead!
Dear as the blood ye gave;
No impious footstep here shall tread
The herbage of your grave;
Nor shall your story be forgot,

While Fame her record keeps,
Or Honor points the hallowed spot
Where Valor proudly sleeps.

Yon marble minstrel's voiceless stone
In deathless song shall tell,
When many a vanished age hath flown,
The story how ye fell;
Nor wreck, nor change, nor winter's blight,
Nor Time's remorseless doom,
Shall dim one ray of glory's light
That gilds your deathless tomb.

Appendix D

Premier Cemetery Service Corporation

Premier Cemetery Service Corporation, a privately owned company under contract with the State of Texas, is charged with operating and maintaining Texas' four state veterans cemeteries in Killeen, Mission, Abilene, and Corpus Christi.

Through these contracts, Premier is committed to providing services that meet or exceed the expectations of all veterans and their families, the US Department of Veterans Affairs, the National Cemetery Administration, the Texas General Land Office, and the Texas Veterans Land Board.

Those services include:

> Honoring all veterans with a final resting place that provides a lasting tribute worthy of their services to a grateful nation;
>
> Serving all veterans and their families with the utmost dignity, respect, and compassion;
>
> Providing an institution that inspires visitors to understand and appreciate the service and sacrifice of our nation's veterans; and
>
> Maintaining each cemetery as both a state and national shrine, sacred to the honor and memory to those interred or memorialized there.

In 1974, Gene Bagwell formed Maintenance Management Company (MMC) to provide custodial services to municipal and corporate entities. Having done this for three years, he expanded MMC's role to include grounds maintenance and horticultural services.

By 1980, Bagwell had expanded MMC's services a second time to include cemetery grounds maintenance after he acquired the City of San Marcos, Texas, cemetery maintenance contract. Five years later, San Marcos broadened the scope of its contract with MMC to include administration over burial properties and services. In 1990, the City of San Marcos further extended its agreement to include "turnkey" administrative services.

Due to his success in San Marcos, Bagwell and MMC were awarded a contract with the City of Austin, Texas, to manage and operate its five municipal cemeteries. With this, he created InterCare Corporation (ICC). However, after realizing the need for quality burial services, he created Interment Services Incorporated (ISI) in 1995. Working with its sister company, ICC, ISI began providing interment and related graveside services in Austin and the surrounding communities.

In March 2005, Bagwell once again expanded his corporate structure by creating a new company—Premier Cemetery Service Corporation. Tailored specifically to work as a partner with the Texas General Land Office and the Texas Veterans Land Board, Premier works toward meeting the state's mission of serving Texas' nearly two million veterans by managing and operating each of the four state veterans cemeteries.

Appendix E

Emblems of Belief for Government Headstones

AVAILABLE EMBLEMS OF BELIEF

Emblem (98) MUSLIM (Islamic 5-Pointed Star) is not shown due to copyright.

Appendix F

Floral and Grounds Policies at National Veterans Cemeteries

Fresh-cut flowers are permitted on graves year round. Flowers may be removed to facilitate cemetery operations such as lawn mowing and grounds maintenance.

Flower pick-up dates are posted on “Next Flower Pick-Up” signs posted at cemetery entrances. During flower pick-up dates, all items will be removed from graves and will not be retained. Persons who placed items on graves may recover those items from their loved one’s gravesites prior to the scheduled pick-up dates.

Artificial flowers may be placed on graves throughout the year but may be removed as soon as they become faded and unsightly.

To preserve the dignity of the cemetery, items placed on graves must be floral in nature. Commemorative items, balloons, pinwheels, glass items, votive or vigil lights, candles, statues, shepherd’s hooks, and stuffed animals are not permitted. Items not permitted on gravesites will be removed from graves to be held in a centralized area on cemetery grounds and will be held for one month prior to disposal. The cemetery staff will assist families in retrieval of the tributes when requested.

Flowers delivered by a florist must have all wrapping paper removed, and no other packing materials may be left at the gravesite.

The cemetery director reserves the right to remove and destroy without notice anything left on graves that violates the intent of these regulations, offends the sensibilities of the public or the dignity of this cemetery, is an eyesore, or is a threat to the safety of the public or cemetery personnel.

Plantings or potted plants will not be permitted on graves at any time.

Christmas wreaths or grave blankets are permitted on graves during the Christmas season from December 1 until January 20 of each year. Grave floral blankets may not be larger than two feet by three feet. Cemetery trees, shrubs, or any other plants may not be decorated with any ornaments of any kind at any time.

Floral items and other types of decorations or objects may not be attached to headstones, markers, or niches at any time.

Plastic or metal vases are permitted only on graves. Cemetery-supplied vases are federal property and are not allowed to be removed from the cemetery. Plastic vases are located in receptacles throughout the cemetery and should be returned to the receptacles when no longer needed.

Glass or easily breakable objects of any kind are not permitted in the cemetery and will be immediately removed.

Headstones are federal property. Altering or marking by paint, marker, lipstick, or any other means is considered vandalism and may be subject to penalty as defined in 38 CFR § 1.218 ("Security and Law Enforcement at VA Facilities").

The national cemetery assumes no responsibility for items left on gravesites. Due to the open nature of the grounds, the cemetery cannot guarantee against theft, vandalism, or the effects of nature. Anyone caught removing items from gravesites not their own will be prosecuted to the fullest extent of the law.

Appendix G

Cemetery Directory

National VA Cemeteries in Texas

Cemetery	Address	Burial
Dallas–Fort Worth National Cemetery	2000 Mountain Creek Parkway Dallas, TX 75211	Open
Fort Bliss National Cemetery	5200 Fred Wilson Road El Paso, TX 79906	Open
Fort Sam Houston National Cemetery	1520 Harry Wurzbach Road San Antonio, TX 78209	Open
Houston National Cemetery	10410 Veterans Memorial Drive Houston, TX 77038	Open
Kerrville National Cemetery	3600 Memorial Boulevard Kerrville, TX 78028	Closed
San Antonio National Cemetery	517 Paso Hondo Street San Antonio, TX 78202	Cremation Only

Texas State Veterans Cemeteries

Cemetery	Address	Burial
Central Texas State Veterans Cemetery	11463 South Highway 195 Killeen, TX 76542	Yes
Rio Grande Valley State Veterans Cemetery	2520 South Inspiration Road Mission, TX 78572	Yes
Texas State Veterans Cemetery at Abilene	7457 W. Lake Road Abilene, TX 79601	Yes
Coastal Bend State Veterans Cemetery	9974 IH-37 Access Road Corpus Christi, TX 78410	Yes

Sources

Primary Sources

The primary sources for this book are observations from multiple visits to the ten veterans cemeteries in Texas during the different seasons of the year and from interviews and correspondence with each director, all of whom made their files and records available.

Photographs

All photographs are by the author.

Maps

Maps of each of the cemeteries were provided by that cemetery's director.

Brochures

Brochures obtained from cemeteries' directors contained information on the history, visitors' guide, floral policies, and burial arrangements. Other information on each cemetery is available by checking cemetery sites on any Internet search engine.

Publications

Books

Abrams, Ronald B., Richard V. Spataro, and Amy F. Odom. *Veterans Benefits Manual 2016 Edition*. New York: LexisNexis, 2016.

Borden, Mariam Edelman, and Peter S. Gaytan. *For Service to Your Country*. New York: Citadel Press, 2011.

Barkley, Roy R., Douglas E. Barnett, and Ron Tyler, eds. *The New Handbook of Texas*. 6 vols. Austin: Texas State Historical Association, 1996.

Holt, Dean W. *American Military Cemeteries*. Jefferson, NC: McFarland, 2009.

Howell, Terry. *The Military.com Guide to Military and Veterans Benefits*. Annapolis, MD: Naval Institute Press, 2017.

Icon Group International. *National Cemetery: Webster's Image and Photographic History, 1865 to 2006*. Rockville, MD: Icon Group International, 2010.

Jordan, Terry G. *Texas Graveyards: A Cultural Legacy*. Austin: University of Texas Press, 1984.

Knudsen, Robert C. *A Living Treasure: Seasonal Photographs of Arlington National Cemetery*. Sterling, VA: Potomac Books, 2008.

MacCloskey, Monro. *Hallowed Ground: Our National Cemeteries*. New York: R. Rosen Press, 1968.

Snyder, Donald C. *National Cemetery System: Opportunities to Expand Cemeteries Capacities*. Darby, PA: Diane Publishing, 1997.

U.S. Senate Subcommittee on Veterans Affairs. *Medal of Honor: 1963–1973*. Washington DC: US Government Printing Office, 1973.

Government Regulations

National Cemetery Administration. *Claim for Standard Government Headstone or Marker (VA Form 40–1330)*. Washington, DC: National Cemetery Administration, 2014.

______. *Interments in Department of Veterans Affairs National Cemeteries*. Washington, DC: National Cemetery Administration, January 2011.

______. *Operational Standards and Measures (States, Territories, and Tribal Organizations)*. Washington, DC: National Cemetery Administration, 2014.

Texas Veterans Land Board. *Policy for Donation of Memorial Plaques and Benches*. Austin: Texas Veterans Land Board, 2016.

______.*Texas State Veterans Cemeteries, Title 40, Part 5, Chapter 178*. Austin: Texas Veterans Land Board, May 23, 2004.

______. *To Honor Those Who Served*. Austin: Texas Veterans Land Board, 2015.

______. *Veterans Land Board Strategic Plan 2016–2018*. Austin: Texas Veterans Land Board, 2016.

Index